Africa's development in the 21st century: Reshaping the research agenda

Fantu Cheru

NORDISKA AFRIKAINSTITUTET, UPPSALA 2008

A background paper commissioned by the Nordic Africa Institute
for the Swedish Government White Paper on Africa.

Indexing terms:
Economic and social development
Sustainable development
Regional integration
Partnership
International economic relations
Globalization
Development strategy
Governance
Democratization
Development research
Africa

The opinions expressed in this volume are those of the author
and do not necessarily reflect the views of the Nordic Africa Institute.

Language checking: Elaine Almén
ISSN 0280-2171
ISBN 978-91-7106-628-2 (print)
ISBN 978-91-7106-632-9 (electronic)
© The author and Nordiska Afrikainstitutet 2008
Printed in Sweden by Elanders Sverige AB, Mölnlycke 2008
Grafisk form Today Press AB

CONTENTS

Introduction

As Africa enters the 21st century, it faces mounting challenges as well as new opportunities. Unlike the in 1980s and the 1990s, however, the conditions for Africa's sustained growth and development are much more favourable today than ever before for four mutually reinforcing reasons. First, despite the social cost of implementing harsh economic reform measures since the early 1980s, many African countries have put in place appropriate macroeconomic, structural and social policies, which have contributed to improved GDP growth rates and some progress towards meeting the Millennium Development Goals. Overall GDP growth rate has averaged in excess of 4.5 percent annually since the mid-1990s. Some of the fastest growing African economies are on course to meet the income poverty target of halving poverty by 2015.

Second, there is greater consensus among Africans now than ever before on what needs to be done to accelerate growth, reduce poverty and promote sustainable development in Africa. Regional initiatives under the African Union (AU) and the New Partnership for African Development (NEPAD) are allowing African countries to improve governance; assume leadership and accountability for their development; increase trade within Africa and the world; and enhance the provision of regional public goods such as cross-country transportation and electricity pooling. Most significantly, these initiatives have resulted in a decline in the number of civil conflicts over the last four years from 16 to 6, including progress on such protracted wars as those in Liberia, Sierra Leone and Angola. The African Peer Review Mechanism, under which a country puts itself up for scrutiny by its peers to help identify its weaknesses and the actions required to correct them underscores the push for accountability in economic and political governance also fueled by an invigorated civil society. So far, more than 25 countries have voluntarily signed up for the NEPAD African Peer Review Mechanism (APRM) and the process has begun with a number of reviews. Moreover, there are encouraging signs that the African Union (AU) and regional bodies are playing an important role in dealing with potentially disruptive national crises, as in the Sudan and Somalia.

Third, while Africa itself deserves the credit for much of what has been achieved, the response of its international partners has been valuable and enhances the prospects for sustaining the progress made so far. In 2005, the international community agreed to double assistance to Africa and to cancel the debt of 14 low income African countries, and the success of the ongoing Doha trade negotiations will be determined in large part by breakthroughs on the issues of particular concern to African countries – the elimination of trade-distorting subsidies in agriculture and the lowering of tariffs and non-tariff barriers for African products. In this context, the Commission for Africa made a compelling case for a "big push" on many fronts to address the interlocking problems standing in the way for successful development to occur in Africa.

Fourth, Africa is already benefiting from an Asia-driven (China in particular) commodity boom and increased investment in infrastructure and the extractive industry sector, followed by investment from India and other East Asian economic powers. Exports are booming and consumer imports more affordable. Net exports of crude oil, wood and precious stones have benefited from strong Asian demand. Financial flows are on the rise as well. China, in particular, has become a large provider of infrastructure loans. Clearly, the rise of the Asian giants, which is likely to be long term, requires that African countries devise innovative responses to the challenges and opportunities it represents. Many questions remain unanswered: How best can Africa benefit from the rise of the Asian giants? What are the risks in economic diversification and transformation? How can these risks be contained?

The strategic challenge: Overcoming embedded dysfunction

While there is good reason to be optimistic about the future of the continent, there are still important challenges. The most pressing issue, one that should be on top of the political agenda, is how to tackle the *widespread poverty and human deprivation*. Africa has the world's highest proportion of poor people (46 percent of the population), and is home to more than 30 percent of the world's poor. The challenge is huge since poverty is multi-dimensional and requires actions and resources on all fronts.

- Vulnerability to hunger remains pervasive.
- Infant and maternal mortality rates, though declining, still remain very high. Many die from simple preventable diseases, such as cholera and diarrhoea. In many places, mortality rates can be cut drastically by simply making it easy for people to have access to clean drinking water.
- Despite considerable progress since the 1960s, 50% of the people in sub-Saharan Africa do not have access to adequate health care. The average expenditure on the health sector rarely exceeds about 5% of GDP.
- Health is also affected by lack of access to clean drinking water and adequate sanitation services. One out of four Africans has access to clean water. The coverage for sanitation is the lowest in the world, with dire consequences for public health, particularly in the crowded slums of African cities.
- Moreover, the HIV/AIDS pandemic remains the greatest threat to African development. The disruptive effects of the epidemic are myriad. The AIDS pandemic is already measurably eroding economic development, educational attainment and child survival – all key measures of national health – in much of Africa.
- Demand for education at all levels is outstripping the supply of educational facilities and resources; spending on education remains low, about an average of USD 25 per annum per person. The female participation rate in schooling remains depressingly low.

Official statistics do not adequately capture the scale of human deprivation in Africa. Even the progress towards the Millennium Development Goals (MDGs) by the best performing countries remains modest at best, and the majority of countries on present trends will take several decades to meet most of the goals. *Economic development and strengthening democratic governance must, therefore, top the political agenda if the continent is to reverse the scale of human deprivation and ecological decline.*

Indeed, the reasons for the slow rate of economic and social progress are many. One key factor has been the persistent *decline in agricultural productivity*. Agriculture, the backbone of African economies, has done comparatively worse than other sectors. Unlike East Asia, there has been no green revolution in African agriculture and the continent is the only region in the world where per capita food self-sufficiency has declined significantly. The poor performance in agriculture is largely due to the pervasive and significant taxation of agriculture in most countries, combined with the crowding out of private investment and production activities through restrictions on market entry and controlled input and commodity pricing. This is in sharp contrast to East Asia where agrarian reform was the major means of redistributing wealth and income, thereby increasing purchasing power and generating high levels of economic growth. Agricultural transformation in turn served as the basis for industrialization, paving the way for a more diversified economic base to emerge.

Compounding the decline in agricultural productivity is the threat posed by *climate change*. Even though Africa has done little to contribute to climate change, it is one region in the world that will be hit hard. With climate change, the seasonal prediction of rainfall has become obsolete, as precipitation patterns have changed completely and become erratic. Water scarcity, land degradation and deforestation, which were already severe, are getting worse and the capacity of national governments to put in place adaptation measures, such as renewable energy technologies and measures to curb deforestation, soil erosion and improper use of water sources, remain weak, if not non-existent.[1] These climatic changes have brought far-reaching effects for the people as livelihood practices, such as pastoralism and subsistence farming – already affected by poor government policies, are severely threatened and are on the verge of collapse.

Expanding *opportunities for gainful employment* remains a critical challenge in Africa where more than fifty percent of the population is under the age of twenty. Across the continent high rates of unemployment, particularly among the youth, who are often poorly educated, are not only a major challenge for economic policy makers but have long-term consequences for aggravating inter-generational transmission of downward poverty spirals. Lack of accessibility and mobility for the majority widens the development gap between the haves and the have-nots and leads to declining opportunity in the social, economic and political spheres. Growing social polarization, therefore, leads to a loss of faith in the system, and consequently to conflict, criminality, anarchy, looting and self-destruction.

The combined effect of poor economic performance, declining soil fertility and ecological collapse of the productive base, and high population growth create the conditions for mass migration, which is already having a major impact on national, regional and global politics and social policy. With declining opportunities for employment and other means to get out of poverty, both educated and unskilled Africans are voting with their feet. Although much of the migration debate centres on South-North migration (i.e. to Europe), a high proportion of African migration is inter-regional, given the porous nature of African borders. This inter-regional migration can put major stress on the resources of host countries who themselves are equally poor. This is particularly the case in sub-regions of Africa that contribute to refugee generating because of internal conflict. In addition to becoming direct actors in these regionalised civil wars, neighbouring states are also involved as hosts to large numbers of forcibly displaced migrants fleeing a complex humanitarian emergency.

One particular aspect of this mass migration with severe consequences for Africa's long-term development is the problem of *brain drain*. It is estimated that as many as 100,000 highly educated Africans leave the continent each year. The loss of skilled people will continue to affect the functioning of the institutions of higher learning, health systems, industry and enterprises. It creates in tertiary institutions a huge vacuum through the lack of experienced leaders for the development and training of younger cohorts. This is particularly most acute in the departure of health professionals – nurses and doctors – and this has a crippling effect on health

---

1. Holmberg, 2007.

services.[2] It is a cruel irony that, sub-Saharan Africa – one of the poorest region in the world, pays the price of producing human capital for use by richer countries while its own development goals are severely constrained by the outflow of scare skilled manpower.[3]

Poor economic performance is also partly attributed to the pervasive *democratic deficit* that characterizes much of Africa. Post-independence African governments have failed to create the necessary 'enabling environment' for sustained and inclusive development to take place. The task was made even more difficult by the post-independence international political environment, in the context of the Cold War that restricted African choices for 'political manoeuvre'. With the end of the Cold War, however, a new momentum was created that opened up avenues for democratic expression in Africa. While democracy as an idea has triumphed in much of the continent since 1990, in practice it is in profound trouble. All too often, elections deteriorate to the formal legitimation of autocratic rule and diminish the role of civil society. Instead of being liberating, multiparty systems might lead to new forms of old hierarchies. Political leaders seek to pursue power and profit by patterns of bargaining, manipulation, and deceit. This does not build local capacity or national purpose. While multiparty elections and universal suffrage are important formal criteria, they are by no means sufficient to judge the democratic qualities of a society. In impoverished societies such as in Africa, democracy must go beyond free expression and inclusion of diverse groups in national politics. There must be an organic link between political freedom and freedom from hunger, ignorance, and diseases.

Finally, Africa's development has been held back by the lack of significant progress in promoting *gender equality*. Although women make up the majority of the rural poor, their contribution to the household as well as to the society in general is rarely recognized. Women produce the bulk of food and constitute 60–80 percent of the agricultural work force. Yet, women are often economically, socially and politically marginalized. For democracy to succeed in Africa, there must be a firm commitment to a full constitutional guarantee for women to obtain the rights of access to land, education, control of resources and decision-making.

In the pages that follow, the key priority areas of research at the Nordic Africa Institute for the coming five years are discussed briefly. In reshaping the research agenda on Africa, there is recognition that a comprehensive and multidisciplinary approach is needed to tackle the interlocking problems impending Africa's growth and development.

---

2. Adepoju, 2007, p. 30.
3. United Nations, 2006.

1. Rural poverty, food insecurity and the struggle for resources

Despite growing urbanization, the majority of Africans remain either physically located in, or dependent on rural or agrarian environments under conditions of severe or sustained vulnerability. The majority, almost 60 percent, of the rural population have an income below the poverty line. While smallholders constitute 73 percent of the rural population, a significant percentage of rural residents are landless farmers. In acknowledging this, a great deal of attention in development discourse and practice has been geared towards rural "poverty reduction", with various poverty reduction strategies and the Millennium Development Goals being recent examples of this global emphasis.

An emphasis on peasants and peasant production, and on "customary" tenure relations and traditional authorities, has dominated perspectives on "rural Africa". This has tended to mask, downplay or dichotomise more complex and varied dynamics, such as the mobility and links between rural and urban areas and processes of social reproduction more generally. In this sense, notions of the rural or agrarian in contemporary Africa (as well as elsewhere) need to incorporate a much more diverse and changing set of interconnected conditions, relations and dynamics. It is necessary to guard against simplistic assumptions or narrow prescriptions that deepen economic impoverishment and social marginalisation or undermine environmental sustainability.

The changing role of agriculture

Agriculture (encompassing crops, livestock and fisheries) plays a key if complex role in the lives and livelihood generation of Africans across the continent, and continues to be critical to national development despite evidence of massive flight from the countryside and the failure of most rural development policies to stem this trend. As such, "it is pertinent to explore what the current role of agriculture and rural development in African national economies is and its potential for improving material standards of living and life chances. In other words, it is time to ask if agriculture spells welfare enhancement or decline for Africa's rural dwellers".[4]

At the moment, agriculture accounts for about 35% of sub-Saharan Africa's GDP and 70% of employment, and 40% of exports (World Bank 2008). There are at least three different types or scales of agriculture occurring and each requires or generates its own kinds of policies, politics and production and reproduction dynamics. There is large-scale commercial agriculture, which predominates in mainly former settler colonies; small-scale production for markets; and subsistence farming, undertaken mostly for home consumption. Despite the distinctions between scales, types and locations of farming, often associated with different kinds of administrative/tenure arenas, they are all somehow linked to one another historically, economically, socially and politically.

---

4. Havnevik et al., 2007.

The scale and nature of rural poverty in Africa

	Million
Total rural population	337
Total rural population below the poverty line	204
Percent of rural population below the poverty line	60
Percentage of rural populations that are:	
-Smallholder farmers	73
-Landless	11
-Nomadic/pastoralists	13
-Ethnic/indigenous	0.9
-Small/artisanal fishers	3
-Internally displaced/refugees	6
Households headed by women as percentage of rural households	31

Source: FAO, State of World Rural Poverty

With regard to large-scale commercial farming where it exists (mainly in southern and parts of East Africa), this has largely emerged historically out of colonial dispossession of the best agro-ecological lands, and evolved through forms of coerced labour and long-term preferences and privileges for minority commercial farmers, while "under-developing" African farming on marginal lands. At the same time, it has been a key source of employment (albeit at extremely low wage levels) for many (often migrants) without either land or resources to cultivate. Nonetheless, in most parts of Africa, agriculture is still dominated by small-holder production regimes which are largely characterised by the significant role played by women and unequal gender relations, a mixed focus on subsistence production as well as small surpluses for exchange, generally low levels of productivity and high levels of poverty, and deepening environmental and natural resource degradation.

What are the constraints to agricultural productivity in Africa?

Despite the significant role of agriculture in national development, however, African governments have consistently failed to create the proper conditions for an agricultural revolution, which would propel the process of industrialization and social development in the continent. If Africa is to feed itself, reduce poverty, and become competitive in world markets, government policies must undergo fundamental change.

In evaluating the literature on rural development in Africa, one is struck by the almost unanimous conclusion that rural development has frequently fallen victim to a 'lack of political will'. One main reason for this is that rural development, whose time frame is long (a generation or more) has been crowded out of the national agenda by other priorities – national security, import-substitution industrialization and so on – considered by central government authorities to be more pressing. There are also external factors – i.e. the structure of the world economy – that work against the interest of African farmers.

Domestic policy factors

The key deficiencies in public policy, which limit the capacity of peasants to escape the trap of poverty and under-production, include:

• *Land scarcity, insecure tenure and landlessness*

Perhaps the most important non-technical issue constraining agriculture in Africa is limited access to land and insecure tenure. The traditional communal land ownership system has given way to individualized private ownership. Land survey departments have come into the picture and the registration of land on an individual basis is spreading. The emergence of new property systems and markets affects social and cultural meanings and dynamics in the long term. With growing pressures towards modernisation, commercialisation, and formalisation, a growing number of peasants are being driven away from their means of existence as land grabbing by powerful forces intensifies.

Another crucial issue related to agrarian change, and shifting property and resource relations, concerns the existence of adequate democratic conditions that may combine the potential for rural material and economic surplus generation with meaningful social and cultural change. In this context, the question is which social forces or actors have authority and capacity to identify and promote change in a positive direction. In imagining "rural" and "agrarian" environments and attempting to understand how they get reshaped, it is important to consider how people organize to change the conditions of their lives. As such, one might do well to question, "How decisions are made and contested over who is able to access land-based resources" in such settings and "Whose claims are recognized, by whom, on what grounds, and where, is of vital importance in the study of African countryside."[5]

• *Inadequate support services and infrastructure*

Productivity decline in African agriculture is largely attributed to the lack of support services and infrastructure. Inadequate training, lack of improved seed, fertilizers and other inputs, and inadequate marketing outlets due to poor roads and transportation have all had a negative impact on the productivity of peasant farmers. Efforts to modernize agriculture have been highly selective in that they have focused on high-potential areas with higher and more reliable rainfall as opposed to lower-potential areas; and on farmers with more resources, the so-called progressive farmers and commercial farmers.

There has also been insufficient attention to technological modernization. There has been little effort to link national technology policy to meeting the needs of the agricultural sector, with a clear focus on supplying intermediate technologies and basic inputs, as the Asian NICs did in the early phase of their development. Investment in research and development has been neglected. Whatever little technological modernization has taken place is exclusively limited to large commercial agricultural estates, and the technology used there is exclusively imported from outside.

• *Inadequate marketing, storage and transport*

Agricultural productivity is also affected by the lack of efficient transport and communication systems and diverse marketing channels. The isolation of African farmers from major domestic and global markets retards agricultural development by increasing transport costs, inhibiting technological adoption, raising the cost of agricultural and social services, and suppressing competitive product, factor and credit markets. Moreover, state monopoly of marketing channels limits the ability of farmers to get premium prices for their products, thus creating disincentives for maximum production.

---

5. Rutherford, 2007.

An additional constraint has been the lack of proper storage facilities. Although the situation varies from region to region, small farmers end up losing a significant amount of harvested crops to pests. Research in and demonstration of alternative and cost-effective methods of storage are in short supply.

• *Gender disparities in rural development*
Rural women play a significant role in agricultural production in Africa. They provide the bulk of labour for planting, weeding, winnowing, storage and marketing. Yet they remain invisible to play makers and extension advisors. They lack access to productive assets, particularly land. The customary systems typically prohibit women's direct access to land, either by ownership or inheritance. Efforts to reform these laws have been made at the margin, leaving untouchable the customary prohibitions (Butwega, 1991). Even when women have access to land, much discrimination is observed in the provision of agricultural education, training, extension, and credit. Programmes to increase food production in Africa must, therefore, reach women if they are to succeed.

• *Excessive rent seeking by the state*
Excessive state interference and the maintenance of inappropriate macroeconomic and trade policies have been at the core of the productivity decline in African agriculture. Overvalued currencies, restrictive exchange rate regulation, and high taxes have historically adversely affected rural economies, undermining productivity at the farm level. Excessive rent seeking by the state further compounds the problem as transaction costs for farmers far exceed their investments. At the centre of this process are the marketing boards that are considered symbols of exploitation. Prices paid to farmers for food crops are kept artificially low, thus providing cheap food to people in the cities (Bates, 1981; World Bank, 1981).

Declining agricultural output in Africa is, therefore, part of a wider pattern whereby African governments, regardless of their ideological persuasion, have consistently failed to recognize the role of small farmers when setting their development priorities. Government investment strategies across the continent have tended to favour projects in urban areas or in highly mechanized export agriculture. The needs of the majority of subsistence farmers are rarely addressed. It is therefore not surprising that many farmers have "voted with their feet" by increasingly engaging in non-agricultural livelihoods or migrating to urban areas, or engaging in other forms of "de-peasantisation" or "de-agrarianisation".[6] There exists a paradox of decreasing returns from farming and increasing "de-agrariansiation" on the one hand, alongside intensified struggles over land on the other. This latter situation raises critical issues about the multiple material and symbolic qualities of "land" beyond its agricultural or productive potential, which connects with interweaving questions of identity, belonging and citizenship for both rural and urban Africans under conditions of growing insecurity and uncertainty. All of the above has great relevance for how land and agrarian reforms need to be conceptualised.

External constraints
• *Unfavourable global market*
A majority of African countries are commodity-dependent, in that 50% or more of their exports are composed of non-oil commodities and most of these are agricultural commodities. Firstly this makes these countries highly vulnerable in relation to changing world markets in

---

6. De-agrarianization is defined by Bryceson (2002) as "a long-term process of occupational adjustment, income-earning reorientation, social identification and spatial relocation of rural dwellers away from strictly agricultural-based modes of livelihood."

which agro-commodity prices, especially for "tropical" commodities, have been systematically declining in recent decades. Under increasingly polarised global commodity conditions, the share of African countries in world commodity trade is declining, alongside their capacity to diversify into higher value commodities or manufacturing.

The persistent decline of commodity prices, despite rapid expansion in production, is influenced by many factors. Many primary resource products are facing mounting competition from substitutes such as synthetics for cotton, aluminium for copper, and sugar beet and corn syrup for cane sugar. Secondly, in the cases of meats, grains, sugar, oilseeds and cotton, the developed countries (i.e. the EU Common Agricultural Policy) have stimulated over-supply as a result of their own domestic subsidy systems. This in turn contributes to global oversupply and declining prices. Notwithstanding this decline in commodity prices, however, African economies have not made the necessary switch from reliance upon primary export commodities.

In the final analysis, the combination of internal processes of agrarian change as well as global dynamics of integration and economic liberalisation means that rural forms of production and reproduction are gradually developing in novel directions. These processes may accelerate if recent suggestions to grow export crops for bio-fuels are implemented. In addition, new "agrarian actors" are entering the scene, such as urban-based elites investing in rural land. All this makes it especially important to root an understanding of dynamic rural environments and agrarian change in historically grounded and spatially specific research.

Transforming African agriculture: The way forward

The majority of Africans remain either physically located in, or dependent on, rural or agrarian environments. Nevertheless the old rural/urban dichotomy is becoming increasingly irrelevant. A focus on links and mobility between rural and urban areas is needed. Also current processes of change create new dynamics of exclusion and belonging. Increased resource competition creates new contestations between men and women and between young and old, utilizing frictions and fissures between customary and statutory laws, and between informal and formalised logics.

Understandings of resource and property regimes have so far led to several different kinds of responses to lessen or alleviate conflicts. These responses include community-based initiatives, as well as local and state co-management of forests, game reserves, and national parks. However, options for resolving resource conflicts or lessening competition in sustainable ways require an appreciation of the co-existence of multiple authorities within rural settings. In light of this, it is necessary to acknowledge and maintain alternative spaces and opportunities for rural producers to voice their interests and needs from below.

Indeed, the priority task of agricultural revolution is obviously complex and multifaceted. At the minimum, it requires the presence of a strong and effective "enabling state", with the capacity to respond effectively to the demands of rural producers. While the state in Africa has been part of the problem, it would be a mistake to underestimate its critical role in any effective rural development strategy. The crucial challenge is how to dismantle the "disabling state' and replace it with 'a state, which is not only protector and supporter, but also enabler and liberator" (Chambers, 1991:20). As experience from East Asia has shown, the state must play an active and supporting role by investing in agricultural research, extension, transport and communications and storage facilities which are essential factors for raising productivity and increasing income for the poor. Government guaranteed prices and security of land tenure in particular are the most effective incentives.

Finally, despite the unwarranted assumption that the continent's destiny is necessarily rooted in peasant agriculture, the population is actually becoming less agrarian in nature for many reasons (Bryceson, 2002). Environmental degradation and a real threat from climate change are major driving forces in this process besides other reasons. Therefore, greater attention must be given to *generating and expanding employment in non-agricultural sectors* through diversification of the rural economy. This is arguably an even greater challenge for development than the technical rehabilitation of agriculture itself. At the centre of rural diversification is rural industrialization. Public policy should be reoriented to provide incentives for the establishment of small and medium-scale rural industries to serve the needs of rural people for services, capital goods, agricultural inputs and agricultural processing, as well as basic consumer goods. These activities, while providing gainful employment, would strengthen the internal working of the national economy by stimulating production and consumption of local goods and services.

2. The urban challenge in Africa

Introduction

Like many other regions in the world, sub-Saharan Africa is confronted with the challenge of rapid urbanization in the context of economic stagnation, poor governance, decrepit urban infrastructure and weak public institutions. By the year 2010, it is estimated that approximately 55% of Africans will be residing in cities (UNDP, 1991:1). This rapid urban growth has brought with it a host of problems, including unemployment and underemployment, a burgeoning informal sector, deteriorating infrastructure and service delivery capacity, overcrowding, environmental degradation, and an acute housing shortage. The rapid expansion in urban population has occurred without the needed expansion in basic services and a dynamic urban economy capable of producing adequate employment opportunities. The problem is compounded by weak urban government structures with very limited capacity to stimulate economic growth, mobilize resources and provide the most basic services.

Despite these alarming trends, there is a persistent tendency by development planners to focus solely on rural poverty. Policy makers have tended to equate urban life with a small group of national elites who govern the country. In his persuasive book from 1977, *Why Poor People Stay Poor: Urban Bias in World Development*, Michael Lipton argued that to invest in urban areas is to undermine rural development, the mainstay of many developing countries (Lipton, 1977). This argument has helped shape the anti-urban bias in African development strategies, which continues today. The result has been a neglect of the particular problems of the majority of urban dwellers, especially the poor who live in squatter settlements or slums (Lee-Smith and Stren, 1991:23–36).

The anti-urban bias goes against the prevailing view that sees urbanization as a progressive process and as one of the key forces underlying technological innovation, economic development and socio-political change. Urbanization has been found to have positive impacts on fertility, mortality and other demographic trends. The current resurgence of interest in and attention to urban management, and the view that cities are the engines of national economic growth and development in general, is in part, based on this pro-urban perspective. This is particularly true today in a knowledge-intensive globalizing economy where cities have played a central role as agents of innovation diffusion and socio-economic transformation.

This report attempts to highlight the key issues in African urban dynamics that require urgent action by researchers and policymakers in order to institute innovative interventions by national governments and local authorities if African urban centres are to become a locomotive for growth.

Key Dimensions of the Urban Crisis in Africa

Most cities in Africa are experiencing deepening and cumulative patterns of inequality. These inequalities predate the current phase of globalization, but are further reinforced by globalization processes of the post-1980s. Increased competition among cities to attract capital and businesses for generating employment and sources of tax revenues has led to widening inequalities between cities and social groups within cities (Hoogevelt, 1997).

Since the early 1980s, large numbers of African countries have had to implement market-oriented economic and institutional reforms under the watchful eyes of the IMF and the

World Bank. Public provision of basic services – the hallmark of the developmentalist theories of the 1950s–1970s – has particularly been targeted for major restructuring, bringing it in line with a market-oriented approach. On the pretext of increasing efficiency and reducing cost, such reforms were used to dismantle the historic construct of the state as a developer (World Bank, 1993). Yet, the promised advantages of economic restructuring – efficiency and cost reduction in the provisioning of basic services – have not been borne out. Instead, poverty, mass unemployment, and inequality have mushroomed. These inequalities are manifested in the following ways:

Increased urban-rural imbalance

There are sharp disparities between the urban and rural areas of Africa. The rural areas have become marginalized from the mainstream of national development. Low levels of agricultural production, the lack of non-farm employment opportunities, and the absence of vibrant small and medium-sized urban centres facilitating interaction between rural areas and major cities, and the disparities in the level of services provided collectively accentuate the rural exodus to primate cities (Gilbert and Gugler, 1992:49–65). It is estimated that, by the year 2020, over 55 percent of Africans will be living in cities (UN-Habitat, 2003). Increasingly, a large percentage of migrants are youth, who often find themselves exposed to exploitation and abuse in their new environment. Only a small minority succeeds in finding gainful employment. Once migrants reach the city, however, they confront some of the same conditions of low productivity, joblessness, and poor income that they encountered in rural areas, now compounded by overcrowding, pollution, and other urban problems.

The most significant rural-urban imbalance can be seen in the disparities in the provision of basic services. Access to basic services, infrastructure, education and health are unevenly distributed between capital cities and their rural hinterlands. For example, in 2002, 55 percent of urban residents had access to sanitation compared to 25 percent of rural Africans. For drinking water, 39% of urban households have water connection compared to 4 % of households in rural areas (UNICEF/WHO, 2004:310).

A striking difference between middle-income Asia (particularly the NICs) and Africa is that the engine of agricultural production – the mainstay of African economies – is simply not sufficiently powered to increase growth and employment. Besides excessive rent-seeking, post-independent governments have failed to develop small market towns, with the transport-communication infrastructure, and appropriate political-administrative structures necessary to kick-start an agricultural revolution in Africa (Baker, 1992). Low agricultural productivity in turn leads to poor conditions of life in rural areas, further compelling people to migrate to the cities.

Growing poverty and inequality

A large proportion of Africans today live in absolute poverty. Increasingly, however, poverty is becoming an urban phenomenon and is growing rapidly (Satterthwaite, 1995:3–10; Sparr, 1994; UN-Habitat, 2006). The causes of urban poverty are interlinked, stemming from such factors as *employment insecurity,* sub-standard housing, poor health, low levels of income generation, vulnerability to market shocks, and limited education (Becker, 1994; Amis, 1995; Moser, 1995; Wratten, 1995). Yet, until very recently, the scale and depth of urban poverty were generally underestimated by governments and international agencies because of their preoccupation with defining poverty based on a 'poverty line' income, which tends to underestimate the dimensions of poverty. Poverty lines do not identify who is lacking adequate water and sanitation, or secure accommodation and health care.

Growing differences and competition, which are reflected in residential location, social mobility, and quality of life all tend to increase *segregation*. This segregation manifests itself in the vast differences in the levels of service infrastructure that is accessible to residents of poor neighbourhoods versus those of the upper- to middle-income areas of any city. The poor living in informal settlements typically lack access to municipal electricity, water, transportation, sewage and garbage collection services (UN-Habitat, 2003:216). Drawing from the Johannesburg example, Beall writes "changing patterns of residential polarization are increasingly associated with shifting trajectories of economic development in the city, resulting in new geographies of exclusion" (Beall, 2002:49). Social and spatial fragmentation of many African cities has socio-economic, environmental and political repercussions, including rising violence, urban unrest, environmental degradation and underemployment, which threaten to diminish any gains income and poverty reduction.

The failure to address these problems at the municipal level frequently results in the exacerbation of intra-city tensions, community alienation, erosion of social cohesiveness and overall demoralization. As both the physical and conceptual divisions between urban communities become more acute, a concern for social cohesion and traditional community values is replaced by a narrow focus on overall economic growth. This orientation of priorities ultimately reduces the capacity of a municipal government to fully recognize and successfully address the diverse needs of constituencies (Rees, 1999:22–52).

Increasing informalization of the economy

An important dimension of change in urban Africa pertains to a deep transformation in the sphere of employment and livelihood. As access to secure wage work opportunities declines in most countries in the region, the urban informal sector has become a powerful force for employment creation in virtually all African cities. Although reliable statistics are hard to come by, the proportion of the urban labour force employed in the informal sector has increased dramatically since the economic crises of the 1980s (ILO, 1973; Bromley, 1978:1033–1039; de Soto, 1989).

The urban poor are organizing themselves to meet their shelter needs, mobilize funds to build roads, clinics, and their own rotating credit systems to start up a whole range of businesses, including urban agriculture, in spite of the fact that formal municipal regulations try to outlaw these activities. In many cities, the poor have begun to diversify their earnings by engaging in urban agriculture, defying restrictive land-use controls, and paving the way for more diverse use of urban space; the spontaneous growth of illegal settlements and of petty commodity production; and the maintenance of rural economic links and regional and cultural identities on the part of urban migrants (Cheru, 1989; Jamal and Weeks, 1988:271–292). As a result, the economic and cultural differences between city and rural areas have become blurred (Vitkovic and Godin, 1998). Remittances are very important components of many rural economies and household survival mechanisms, providing a critical source of capital. Declining urban incomes and increases in poverty are beginning to have a significant impact on such flows and on rural change (Amis, 1995: 155). Through collective action, the losers in global restructuring attempt to rewrite the rules governing urban political economy in their favour.

Proliferation of Slums

The growth of slums in the last 15 years has been unprecedented. In 1990, there were nearly 715 million slum dwellers in the world. By 2000, the slum population had increased to 912 million and is approximately 998 million today. UN-Habitat estimates that if current trends continue, it will reach 1.4 billion by 2020. One of every three city dwellers lives in slum conditions; some slums become less visible or more integrated into the urban fabric as cities develop and income improves, while others become permanent features of the urban landscape.

Sub-Saharan Africa hosts the largest proportion of the urban population residing in slums (71.9 percent); 166 million out of a total urban population of 231 million are classified as slum dwellers. The region has the second largest slum population in the world after South-Central Asia, which has 263 million, making up 58 percent of the global urban population (UN-Habitat, 2003). Slum life often entails enduring some of the most intolerable housing conditions, which frequently include sharing toilets with hundreds of people, living in overcrowded and insecure neighborhoods, and constantly facing the threat of eviction. Slum dwellers are also more likely to contract water-borne diseases, such as cholera and typhoid, as well as opportunistic ones that accompany HIV/AIDS. Slum life therefore places enormous social and psychological burdens on residents, which often leads to broken homes and social exclusion.

Although there is a growing recognition worldwide of the need to address the slum question, as manifested in the recent United Nations Millennium Declaration (MDG 7, target 11 – to improve the lives of at least 100 million slum dwellers by 2020), there is still a general apathy and lack of political will among governments to implement policies aimed at improving their living conditions. Without sustained political will and commitment by governments, it will be difficult to reduce the proliferation of slums. Moreover, many past responses to the problem of slums have been based on the erroneous belief that provision of improved housing and related services, through slum upgrading, and physical eradication will on their own, solve the problem. Solutions based on this premise have failed to address the underlying causes of slums, of which poverty is the most significant. Policies should, instead, address the issue of the livelihoods of slum dwellers and the urban poor in general. This means enabling urban informal activities to flourish, linking low-income housing development to income generation, and ensuring easy access to jobs through pro-poor transport and low-income settlement location policies.

Deficiencies in infrastructure and basic services

As African cities have continued to grow in size, their declining economic situation has led to dramatic deterioration in the supply of basic infrastructure and urban services. The breakdown in public transport service, refuse collection, road maintenance, drainage clean up, electricity and water connections, has in turn affected urban productivity as well as the well-being of urban residents (Stren, 1989:36–37; Onibokun, 1989:68–111; Kuluba, 1989: 203–245). The resources necessary for roads, sewers, water systems, schools and hospitals cannot keep up with the needs of the growing urban population. This has spread existing services and infrastructure even more thinly.

The most visible manifestation of the urban crisis in Africa is the lack of access to basic water and sanitation for the poor. Despite the importance of water and sanitation in the fight against poverty, however, African governments have paid scant attention to the need to formulate an appropriate framework to guide the water and sanitation sector and to accelerate investment in order to expand service delivery effectively and efficiently. Low cost water and sanitation receive only between 1% (sub-Saharan Africa) to 3% (Latin America and the Caribbean) of government budgets (IMF/Paris21, 2000). Water and sanitation budgets, which normally fall under the environment ministry, struggle for allocations, especially where basic social services such as education and health are prioritized. With what little investment there is, the scope of coverage and the efficiency of the delivery mechanism have been far below what is adequate (Davis et al., 2003).

In addition to the urban water supply problem, provision of adequate sanitation is perhaps the most critical problem in many African cities. For example, over half of the households in Addis Ababa, Ethiopia had neither private nor shared toilet facilities in 1997, resulting in an indiscriminate use of drains, open spaces and waterways where people also wash. Another 25 percent share pit latrines with other families (Yared, 1996). Emptying of latrines is a problem in most towns due to the absence of desludging vehicles (vacuum trucks). Addis Ababa's first sanitary sewer system serves only the commercial areas and perhaps 15 percent of the higher income population. Water-borne sanitation, however, will remain unaffordable to the vast majority of households for many years to come.

As water scarcity became severe and the marginal cost for supplying rose steeply, national governments and municipalities increasingly turned away from public provision of basic services in the 1980s. But, privatization has neither reduced costs nor expanded the coverage of water supply to previously unserved communities (Jaglin, 2002:231–245). Indeed, higher costs to, and service cut-offs of, persons unable to pay higher rates have become more common. The emphasis on cost recovery has produced a situation whereby those who are too poor to pay are denied basic services. Furthermore, privatized monopolies are reluctant to apply cross-subsidies to meet the needs of those residents who cannot pay the full cost for water supply (UN-Habitat, 2003: ch. 5). As a result, the urban poor are overexposed to environmental risks and life threatening diseases associated with inadequate water provision: diarrhoea, cholera and other water-borne diseases.

Growing health and environmental crisis

In most African countries, the urban poor are over-exposed to environmental risk and life threatening diseases that are preventable. Existing environmental infrastructure is woefully inadequate for providing clean drinking water or hygienically treating household liquid and solid wastes, much less minimizing or treating hazardous and toxic industrial waste. Low income areas not serviced by access roads often wallow in pools of open sewage, mountains of stinking garbage since trucks cannot get there and drainage channels hardly exist (Cheru, 1992).

In cities and neighborhoods with inadequate provision of water and sanitation, mortality rates are commonly 10 to 20 times higher than neighborhoods well served by piped water and sanitation (Pruss et al, 2002). The occurrence of malaria and cholera, often associated with poor rural areas, has now become a common feature of many urban centres in Africa. In the 1990s, for example, cities including Nairobi, Lusaka and Addis Ababa experienced outbreaks of cholera, malaria and other communicable diseases due to poor water and sanitation services. The effects of structural adjustment programmes in many African countries have further accentuated the growing health and environmental crisis as public provision of essential services was replaced with private provision in the name of efficiency and minimizing costs.

In addition to poor water and sanitation services, each day liquid waste (including toxic substances and industrial waste) is disposed of using inadequate on-site methods. Airborne particulate readings in the developing world are often ten times higher than the peak levels allowed in the United States. This situation endangers the health and productivity of the urban poor, especially women and children (World Commission on Environment and Development, 1987; Cairncross et al., 1990; Levey, 1992:134–149).

The resources that municipalities need to provide minimum acceptable levels of basic services, maintain water supply systems and existing fleets of garbage trucks are severely limited. This can be particularly severe when responsibility for water and sanitation service delivery is decentralized to local administrations without the corresponding devolution of financial authority. For instance, only 22 percent of the solid waste in Dar es Salaam was collected in 1988 as a result of the lack of refuse trucks (Kulaba, 1989:236–237). In the late 1980s, the municipality of Addis Ababa, Ethiopia had as many as 40% of the fleet of garbage trucks inactive at any given time for lack of spare parts.

It is difficult to imagine how significant progress can be made for many of the Millennium Development Goals (MDGs) without first ensuring that poor households have a safe, reliable water supply and adequate sanitation facilities. This will require efforts from many parties. Much of the workload rests on governments at local and national levels. But they are not alone. Civil society, the private sector and external donors will have roles to play. All of these actors need to find new resources and improved ways of working together (Global Water Partnerships, 2003).

Poor governance and weak municipal institutions

Despite the growing economic importance of the cities in national development, the policy and institutional framework for managing urban growth in many African countries remains weak or inhospitable. In addition to the persistence of inappropriate macroeconomic policies at the national level, central government control of national development policy has paid little attention to critical responsibilities of local government institutions, such as operation and maintenance of infrastructure, and the establishment of an incentive and enabling legal environment for private economic actors to operate.

The problem of central control has been compounded by weak capacity in municipalities to plan and manage urban development in a sustainable way. What passes for planning at the municipal level are rudimentary forms of land-use, zoning, and licensing regulations, exclusively concerned with limitations and regulations, instead of enabling and empowering local communities (Bubba and Lamba, 1991:37–59). In many cities, current by-laws restrict a host of economic activities because the activities are considered traditional, etc. Housing codes and zoning regulations – inherited from the colonial administration – outlaw certain types of housing and business activities (Lee-Smith and Stren, 1991:23–26). These legal and regulatory environments hamper the productivity and resourcefulness of poor urban residents. As a result, the enormous economic potential of African cities remains untapped.

Diminishing Municipal Revenue Base

How can cities pay for and maintain infrastructure given that the benefits of infrastructure are long-term, fiscal pressures are frequently immediate, and the pressure of the local electoral cycle is short-term?

Like many US cities, urban areas in Africa suffer severe fiscal distress. This became obvious in the 1980s, characterized as the "decade of adjustment". Shrinking revenues were matched by expanding responsibilities. How to pay for new infrastructure investment, provide affordable services without fiscal distress, recover costs, and improve administrative efficiency are all daunting but not insurmountable challenges.

The fiscal crisis of African cities is compounded by failure to solve the central government-local government jurisdictional issue. Central governments have tended to institute and maintain significant financial, legal and regulatory controls, leaving little room for innovation by local authorities (Attahi, 1989:112–146; World Bank, 1991:25; Warah, 2000:8–9). Municipalities lack the the powers required for effective political and economic decision making, particularly in such critical areas as investment in urban infrastructure, service delivery, revenue generation, and promoting urban economic development. Where central governments do not allow municipal authorities to tax or borrow, and yet hold them responsible for provision of services, non-delivery is the end result.

Lack of municipal autonomy prevents local authorities from tapping into Foreign Direct Investment in the water and sanitation sector. While there has been a marked increase in the level of Foreign Direct Investment in the water and sanitation sector over the past two decades, it is unevenly distributed. Silva et al. show that, between 1990–1997, $24.9 billion was invested by the private sector in 97 water and sewerage projects in developing countries: East Asia ($11.9 billion); Europe and Central Asia ($1.5 billion); Latin America ($8.2 billion); and the Middle East ($3.2 billion). By contrast, sub-Saharan Africa received a paltry $37 million involving 8 projects (Silva et al., 1998). Empowering local authorities to run their own affairs can help unlock FDI in the water and sanitation sector.

Finally, the financing gap in the water and sanitation sector is further hampered by the heavy debt burden that many African countries suffer from. The continued outflow of badly needed resources in the form of debt service payment undermines the capacity of national countries to cope with the devastating health impact of cholera, diarrohea and other communicable diseases that are so prevalent in crowded urban centres and slums. Full cancellation of poor countries' debt could produce additional resources that can be directed toward improving water and sanitation delivery in the urban areas of Africa.

Conclusion

The spatial and institutional patterns identified above in turn generate social polarization, between rich and poor, between urban and rural areas, and between different cities. In socio-cultural terms, tensions also exist between poor and rich and between racial and ethnic groups. Local authorities are, therefore, being pressed from above by the invisible forces of globalization, and from below by social force that are losing out in the process of market-oriented economic reforms. Different cities and different communities within them are responding to the challenges posed by globalization in different ways. It is important to capture alternative urban management practices in different cities around the world and testing their effectiveness in protecting promoting and fulfilling the right to adequate housing.

In addition, spatial and social fragmentations have serious implications for urban growth and competitiveness (Halfani, 1989). The lack of foreign investment, negligible involvement in international trade, and the steep decline in export revenues coupled with limited domestic savings and investments imply that the African region cannot share the same technological advances attained in the modern era which are mostly urban based. Ultimately, globalization ends up reinforcing the pre-existing process of 'urbanization without development' whereby inequality and fragmentation continue to worsen, setting the stage for the breakdown of the social order, and making African cities ungovernable.

3. Conflict prevention and post-conflict transformation

Introduction

The African continent has been a region where protracted conflicts have claimed the lives of millions of people over the past twenty-five years. While the roots to these conflicts date back to the colonial period, Africa's longest and most deadly conflicts were fuelled by superpower rivalries. The most deadly conflicts, such as Liberia, Sierra Leone, and Angola have ended. But the legacies of these conflicts are still being felt long after their termination. These conflicts continue to have far-reaching, long-term and varied effects for different groups in Africa, not only in immediately neighbouring states but also in whole regions. More significant is the fact that violent conflict systematically diverts scarce national resources from development, making the recovery stage much more difficult and challenging. These challenges include:

The challenge of reintegration of displaced persons after war

One of the most visible effects of war is mass displacement of civilians. Over the past fifteen years, the African continent has hosted about half of the world's displaced people. In 2000, for example, one-fifth of Africans lived in countries severely disrupted by wars or civil conflicts, and about 90 percent of the casualties were civilians. There were more than 3 million refugees and 16 million internally displaced persons (World Bank, 2000:15). Displacement has been more common in the Horn of Africa, Central Africa and West Africa. The internally displaced, who are much less visible than refugees who cross international borders, comprise between 15 to 20 million people. A worrisome and neglected feature of this pattern is the unusually large proportion of widows and orphans among the displaced.

Forced displacements resulting particularly from civil wars and other major conflicts and crises on the continent are altering the demographic, social, economic, political, cultural and environmental landscapes of many regions. In the process, not only are resources – including bodies, goods, monies and politics – moving across borders (legally and illegally) but border zones themselves are also becoming key sites of both tension and transformation

While the economic costs of displacement (as a result of the abandonment of productive activities) are difficult to calculate, the reintegration and resettlement of millions of returnees and ex-combatants are complex and costly undertakings. Countries emerging from conflict, lacking the financial means and an effective institutional base, are not in a position to undertake the massive task of rehabilitation and reconstruction on their own.

Reactivating the economy and providing basic services

Civil wars not only result in the unprecedented loss of civilian life, but wars also have long-term consequences for development. Hospitals, schools, roads and infrastructures that take decades to build are wantonly destroyed. Food production and marketing systems are also a common casualty of war. Some of the most talented and skilled people are forced to flee to other countries. When the wars finally come to an end, resuming development and normalizing society becomes an even much greater challenge. As is often said, it is easy to destroy in one day what it has taken decades to build. The post-conflict reconstruction challenge is as equally difficult as it is to end the wars in the first place.

Restoring the social fabric and basic institutions of the state

Physical disruption of the habitat and displacement of people often lead to partial or total disintegration of social fabric based on family, clan or tribe. For centuries, these traditional structures have provided cultural roots, preserving Africa's heritage. With the outbreak of conflict, social structures and cultural norms are disrupted. With the demise of traditional cultural structures as a result of conflict, people become vulnerable to cultural 'substitutes' such as religious fanaticism, or political or tribal extremism. How to reconstitute community social capital is perhaps a bigger challenge than the reconstructing of physical infrastructure.

It is clear that once the war ends, re-establishing the development process at the level attained before the commencement of hostilities and building durable peace are very difficult, especially under conditions of economic collapse and with a weak state without the necessary institutions to quickly address the multiple challenges.

Understanding the roots of African conflicts

Understanding conflicts – their roots, practices and persistence – requires attention to a wide range of historical, social, spatial, economic and political processes and dynamics, both local and trans-local. It is important that the complex causes of violent conflict be understood so that policies aimed at ending such conflict and promoting peace can be appropriate and sustainable. In this regard, international actors need to be wary about promoting one-size-fits-all solutions as quick exit strategies from post-conflict societies.

The legacy of the Cold War

Through much of the Cold War period, military rule was the predominant form of government in Africa. Both East and West helped accelerate Africa's militarization by supporting repressive military juntas in face of widespread poverty, denial of civil and political rights, and neglect of infrastructure and social services. With the end of the Cold War, however, two strikingly different realities appeared on the horizon. On the one hand, many long-running conflicts in the continent came to a close when guerrilla insurgents decisively defeated despotic regimes, as was the case in Eritrea and Ethiopia. On the other, the ethnic pieces put together by colonial glue and reinforced by the Old World Order, started to pull apart and began to reassert their autonomy in a handful of African countries with no previous signs of implosion.

It is interesting to note that the worst humanitarian disasters in Africa occurred in countries where dictators played the Cold War game and crushed political dissent in their countries. Valuable American allies during the Cold War, such as Somalia, Liberia and Zaire, splintered along tribal and clan lines as competing warlords waged destructive warfare, which claimed the lives of thousands of innocent civilians, leaving properties and infrastructure destroyed on a massive scale (Human Rights Watch/Africa, 1997). The fall of Siyadd Bare's regime in January 1991 in Somalia, and the 1990 execution of military leader Sergeant Samuel Doe in Liberia by militiamen from Charles Taylor's National Patriotic Front of Liberia, illustrate this point.

Regionalization of conflicts

What distinguishes the wars in Sierra Leone, Liberia and the Democratic Republic of the Congo from other African wars in the past is that they all started out as local level conflicts, but quickly engulfed whole regions and countries for many reasons. These include the in-volvement of neighbouring states in supporting one faction or the other in the conflict, the proliferation of small arms and the mobility of fighters in crossing borders, the artificiality of the borders of African states, the activities of trans-global business interests that extract resources and trade in arms in conflict zones, and refugee movements across borders.

Examples of regionalised conflicts include the "networked wars"[7] of the Mano River area of West Africa, where the Liberian civil war that started in 1989 drew in neighbouring states through "informal trans-boundary networks", contributing to the outbreak of civil war in Sierra Leone in 1991 when rebels, supported by a Liberian rebel leader, invaded the country. Just as the conflicts in Liberia and Sierra Leone were nearing an end at the close of the 1990s, a coup – later followed by civil war – took place in Côte d'Ivoire in 2002, amid reports that some ex-combatants from Liberia and Sierra Leone had been involved in the fighting. The result of this is that the countries in the region – Sierra Leone, Liberia, Côte d'Ivoire, Guinea, Guinea-Bissau and Burkina Faso – have been adversely affected by the con-flicts and have had to contend with serious security challenges. In the same way, the conflict in Nigeria's oil-rich Niger Delta involving insurgent groups has had serious implications not only for the region but also for global energy security.

Similarly, the Great Lakes Region of East and Central Africa was thrown into turmoil following the genocide in Rwanda in 1994 and the outbreak of civil war in the Democratic Republic of the Congo (DRC) in 1997, when Alliance of Democratic Forces for the Libera-tion of Congo-Zaire (ADFL) forces backed by neighbouring Uganda and Rwanda invaded the country and seized power. The subsequent break-up of the alliance led to the expulsion of the erstwhile foreign allies, who then backed new rebel forces and commenced what was later described as "Africa's first world war",[8] involving over seven rebel armies and the na-tional armies from four other neighbouring states.

The regionalisation of civil wars in West, Central and East Africa has posed formidable challenges to regional security as well as global security. Given the trend towards the securi-tization of development, there is a need to re-think and re-focus international engagement with Africa in relation to conflict management and peace building. Central to this is the role of regional organizations, particularly the African Union, civil society organisations and Af-rican citizens themselves.

International response to African conflict after 1989

Many western commentators were quick to point out that the crises in Rwanda, Somalia and Liberia were nothing unusual, just a natural part of the African way of life. Readers of these were even warned in 1994 of 'the coming anarchy' – a new security threat for the western world after the end of the Cold War (Kaplan, 1994). But to describe the genocide in Rwanda and the senseless killings in Somalia as mere 'ethnic conflicts' is a grave error. Clans do not generate conflicts. It is the politicization of clan and ethnic relations, which dates back to colonial policies of 'divide and conquer', that accentuates conflict. Most of the warlords in Liberia and Somalia had little claim to legitimacy of any sort, even among their own clans. They were men who manipulated their clan and ethnic links and their access to arms in order to recruit marginalized youth to fight the former regimes, and to support their struggle for power after the regimes collapsed. They managed to consolidate their brutal political author-

---

7. Duffield, 2002.
8. Nabudere, 2004.

ity, but only after sending millions of innocent people to their deaths and instilling a fear of renewed conflict in the hearts of their people.

Rwanda, Somalia and the failure of the United Nations

The tendency to view African conflicts in 'ethnic terms' was clearly evident in the different reactions of the international community to the tragedies that unfolded in Somalia and Rwanda on the one hand, and on the other, in Bosnia. Support for dispatching a UN military force to the killing fields of Rwanda and Somalia generated little interest in an international community obsessed with Yugoslavia – essentially a crisis involving white people in the heart of Europe. When the Security Council finally approved an emergency airlift of food and the deployment of 500 UN troops to Somalia in July 1992, the Secretary-General Boutros Boutros Ghali, implied that the world's failure to respond to Somalia's plight was rooted in racism.[9]

The indifference towards African conflicts went hand in hand with the failure of the United Nations to intervene expeditiously in crisis spots by failing to commit the needed resources and troops. For example, the Rwandan genocide occurred as a result of the decision by the United Nations to withdraw its peacekeeping forces, against the advice of the head of the UN force in the country. The warning about an impending genocide by UN field commanders three months before the genocide was conveniently ignored by the UN peacekeeping office in New York that was then headed by Kofi Annan, who later became the Secretary-General of the organization in 1996.[10] Apologies by President Clinton and Secretary-General Kofi Annan two years after the genocide were wholly inadequate for both the victims and their surviving relatives.[11]

After the Rwandan genocide: The international community and post-conflict reconstruction

In the aftermath of the Rwandan genocide, peace building and post conflict reconstruction have assumed center stage in the development policies of western bilateral donors and multilateral organizations. There has been a gradual shift from the idea of "conflict resolution" and "conflict management" to the notion of "conflict transformation". "Conflict resolution" implies that conflict is entirely negative, and hence something that should be – and can be – permanently resolved through various forms of management-style intervention or mediation. "Conflict management" assumes that conflicts are longer-term processes that take longer to resolve, but nonetheless envisages that violence and volatility can be resolved and that people can be "managed" or controlled through correct practices without having to address the underlying causes of the problem.[12]

On the other hand, 'conflict transformation', as articulated by successive Secretaries-General of the United Nations, implies a commitment "to enhance respect for human rights and fundamental freedoms, to promote sustainable economic and social development for wider prosperity, to alleviate distress and curtail the existence and use of massively destructive weapons"[13] Within such frameworks, successful peace building requires the recognition of conflict as a dynamic aspect of social life that can be transformed or modified, and that can promote mutual understanding by changing the perceptions of issues, actions and other groups and working

---

9. "The Security Council's Unhumble Servant", *The Economist*, 8–14 August 1992, p. 31.
10. Adelman and Suhrke, 1999.
11. Aronoff, 1998.
12. Lederach, 1995.
13. Annan, 1989.

collectively (and non-violently) towards increased justice and equality in society.

Much of the international community's effort in post-conflict reconstruction over the past decade and half has focussed on important and necessary short-term solutions without having to invest on long-term initiatives that would foster and support sustainable structures and processes.[14] These short-term solutions include: demobilization and ensuring comprehensive disarmament; the reintegration of refugees, displaced persons and ex-combatants; reconstruction and rehabilitation of destroyed infrastructure; establishing and strengthening civil and political administration; and strengthening African regional security structures, such as ECOWAS, IGAD, SADC and the African Union's new Peace and Security Council.[15]

The most effective conflict-prevention strategies in Africa are those described inappropriately as 'post-conflict peace building'. These include: socioeconomic development, capacity building in the area of governance, respect for human rights and political pluralism. A particularly important issue in conflict prevention is how to redress massive economic inequalities and political exclusion. Resolution of the deeper causes of conflict, therefore, requires changes in the social and political order. Regrettably, this monumental agenda has not featured prominently in the post-conflict reconstruction agenda of the international community. This is because the peace building agenda in Africa has become inextricably intertwined with the 'securitization of development' in the post-Cold War, post 9/11 world. Not surprisingly, within this broad interventionist paradigm, international peace building has often been used to promote "a particular vision of how (post-conflict) states should be organised internally – based on the principles of liberal democracy and market oriented economics".[16] Thus a great deal of international support for post-conflict reconstruction in war-torn societies is either implicitly or explicitly ideologically framed to promote a particular type of peace and development.

As is often the case, donor driven post-conflict reconstruction strategies often end up contributing to the re-creation of the very conditions that led to conflict in the first place. A typical example relates to the use of post-war elections as a quick exit strategy for the international community after warring factions sign peace agreements, without addressing the underlying roots of the conflict or acts committed with impunity committed during the war. In both cases of Sierra Leone and Liberia where elections were held following the end of civil wars in 1996 and 1997, the fledging democracies floundered, followed by a regression to civil war.

The role of the international community in peace building and post-conflict transformation must, therefore, come under closer scrutiny. The international community should abandon the delusion that it is responsible for resolving crisis and managing conflict in African countries. For better or worse, peacemaking and peace building are not sustainable unless locals shape the form and content of the processes.

The role of the African Union in conflict prevention
Until very recently, Africa lacked the necessary commitment and organized effort to resolve conflicts. The Organization of African Unity (OAU), the principal pan-African organization, did very little to prevent African conflict, hamstrung by its own outdated principle of non-interference in the internal affairs of member states. The Commission for Mediation, Conciliation and Arbitration remained largely inactive through much of the 1970s and 1980s,

---

14. Bush, 1996.
15. Cheru, 2001.
16. Paris, 2002.

a period when the continent literally bled to death.

Amid such seemingly insurmountable paralysis, Nigeria and South Africa (both regional hegemons) did try to pressure the OAU to become more proactive in conflict prevention and resolution efforts (Le Pere et al., 1999:3–8). Both governments have been very active in a number of initiatives. The Lusaka Peace Accord to end the Angolan civil war was brokered by South Africa while Nigeria's leadership in the Economic Community Monitoring Organization (ECOMOG) to end the Sierra Leone and Liberian civil wars is well known. ECOWAS adopted a protocol formalizing its mechanisms for conflict prevention, management, resolution, peacekeeping and security. Other sub-regional mechanisms such as SADC and IGAD have also adopted similar protocols and conventions to tackle transnational challenges.[17]

While the regional economic communities (RECs) are undertaking peacekeeping, it is also necessary to recognize the work of the African Union, which has stepped up its role in the prevention and management of conflict, particularly through the establishment of the Peace and Security Council (PSC). The PSC is a collective security arrangement to facilitate timely and efficient response to conflicts and crisis situations in Africa. It also functions as the principal organization to promote close harmonization, coordination, and cooperation between regional mechanisms, the Union and the UN system in the promotion and maintenance of peace, stability and security in Africa.

The new security architecture of the AU is very promising and has drawn a lot of international support. The UN is increasingly stepping up its support to African regional peacekeeping operations. Regional forces are mobilized and dispatched to the war affected country as a contingency measure. This force then transitions into a full-blown UN multi-functional peacekeeping and peace building mission, as is the case now with the hybrid-UN regional force in Darfur. The donors have also established the AU Peace Fund to be able to pay for future peacekeeping operations. These are very promising developments which must be sustained over the long term.

Conclusion

The key to sustaining peace in Africa is the localization of the means for conflict resolution. Besides strengthening the African Union and the regional economic communities (RECs) in their response to conflict, civil society must have a central, meaningful role in the efforts to build peace and prevent future conflicts. Governmental, regional and international initiatives will be far more successful if they incorporate the valuable foundation-building work taking place within civil society. In this regard traditional African approaches to conflict resolution cannot be ignored. The AU itself has established a five-member Panel of the Wise consisting of 'highly respected African personalities' to serve as a proactive conflict prevention team. There are many other examples designed to strengthen confidence-building measures and early prevention of conflicts before they get out of control.

Finally, the resolution of the deeper causes of conflict requires changes in the social and political order. This frequently requires constitutional, electoral and judicial reform, reconstruction of the police and armed forces and payment of compensation to victims of arbitrary justice, and addressing structural inequalities that give rise to popular struggles. The bond between peace, democracy and justice must be strengthened.

---

17. Kwesi Aning, 2007.

4. Africa and the World Trading System: The challenge of 'rebalancing' the 'unbalanced rules'

It is widely recognized that international trade can be a powerful engine for a country's socio-economic development. By providing access to foreign exchange, expanding markets, increasing foreign direct investment, facilitating the transfer of technology, and boosting domestic productivity, trade can crate employment and increase domestic incomes. Countries such as China, India, and the East Asian tigers are often pointed out as examples of those who embraced globalization, implemented proper reforms, opened up their economies to foreign investment and trade, thus experiencing rapid growth, and reducing their overall poverty as a result.[18]

In recent years, the conventional assumption that unrestricted free trade can lead to poverty alleviation in developing economies has been criticised for its simplicity. While it is true that the share of developing countries as a group in world trade has increased to around 30 percent in recent years, the benefits have not been distributed evenly. The share of African countries in world trade has generally stagnated. Although a few oil exporting African countries have done well by way of oil export, a *2005 World Trade Report* shows that the majority have witnessed a decrease of their share in world trade. For example, the forty-nine least developed countries (most of which are in Africa), have not shared in the growth of world trade. The 646 million people in the top exporting countries – the US, Germany, Japan, France and UK – have 100 times more trade than their poor counterparts.[19]

There are internal and external factors that contribute to Africa's low participation in international trade. The internal factors include: inappropriate domestic economic and social policies; and lack of progress in regional integration efforts, which has limited the region's ability to reduce transaction costs and increase competitiveness through economies of scale in the development of infrastructure.

On the external front, costly and unfair trading practices of the developed countries have made it difficult for African countries to penetrate export markets in developed countries. Take the case of tariff escalation and developed countries' subsidies. In the case of the first, as long as African countries export unprocessed materials, the tariff remains low. But for every step in the processing chain that adds value, the duties rise sharply. These tariff escalations undermine manufacturing and employment in industries where African countries need to be competitive.

In the case of agricultural subsidies, the developed countries have repeatedly pledged to reduce the size of their farm support. So far the amount of such subsidies has changed little in 20 years while the amount of aid has declined. While the developed countries subsidize their farmers to the tune of 350 billion dollars annually, their development assistance to the poorest countries is barely 50 billion a year.[20]

Africa and the World Trading System

The current international trading system rewards the developed countries disproportionately and creates unmet human needs in the underdeveloped countries. Khor (2001) maintains that the very neo-liberal economic recipes – financial, trade and investment liberalization – that have created enormous wealth in the North have had cataclysmic effects on the South.[21]

18. Dollard and Kraay, 2002.
19. World Trade Organization, 2005.
20. Das, Bhagirath Lal, 2006.
21. Khor, 2001.

In regions like Africa and Latin America, the policies of neo-liberalism are closely associated with economic regression, increased debt, the loss of social services, drastic inequality, declining terms of trade, and financial crisis.

At the launch of the Uruguay Round of Trade Negotiations in the early 1990s, it was argued that a strong-rule based system would benefit smaller and poorer economies by improving their access to northern markets. On the contrary, the benefits of trade liberalization in terms of capital accumulation and productivity growth, balance of payment position, and manufacturing growth tend to be distributed unevenly, and adverse forms of integration into the global economy may actually increase rather than reduce poverty. Despite the elimination of many of the barriers that have restricted international trade in goods, significant barriers to trade still persist – often to the detriment of the poorest countries.

From the Uruguay Round to the Doha Round

The developing countries, especially Africa, have persistently complained that the current international trade regime works against them and have demanded major reform to rebalance the rules. And in 2001, the developed countries agreed to a new round of trade negotiations called the Doha Development Round. The main issue of interest to developing countries in the Doha Round included basic issues of market access to industrial country economies, terms of trade between developing country exports and imports from industrial countries, commodity price volatility and trade patterns, phasing-out export subsidies and trade-distorting domestic support measures in agricultural exports by industrial countries, including especially cotton, and special and differentiated treatment for poor countries.[22] Overall, the terms of trade losses offset about 70% of the official development assistance (ODA), while the loss of market shares in international trade has cost Africa some 68 billion dollars per annum between 1972 and 1997.[23]

Agricultural subsidy

Of all the issues in the current WTO agenda, agriculture has been a hot topic. At the 2001 WTO meeting in Doha, Qatar, governments agreed to create new, fairer trade rules for agriculture by March 2003, and even declared the Doha trade negotiations a 'development round' to put fighting poverty at the heart of the global trade system. The promise then was to eliminate unfair US and EU trade practices that locked African farm products out of rich country markets, yet allowed wealthy nations to flood African markets with massively subsidized exports.

Agricultural subsidy by the developed countries, which is in excess of 350 billion dollars a year, adversely affects the competitive advantage of African farmers, thereby further impoverishing them.[24] One egregious example is the US which spends almost 4 billion dollars on cotton subsidies to 25,000 cotton farmers who produce just 3 billion worth of cotton. The implications of this policy on some African countries which are heavily dependent on cotton exports have been well documented. For instance, cotton production accounts for 5 percent to 10 percent of Gross Domestic Product (GDP) in Benin, Burkina Faso, Chad and Mali.[25] About two million farmers in West and Central Africa produce cotton, accounting for about 30 per-

---

22. Perkins, 2003; Khor, 2004.
23. World Bank, 2000.
24. Das, Bhagirath Lal, 2006.
25. Fortucci, 2003.

cent of total export earnings and more than 60 percent of total agricultural exports.[26] All these countries are low cost producers as opposed to the cotton producers in the EU and the US.

To the extent that subsidies from developed countries continue to dampen commodity prices in the world market, the benefit of trade liberalisation will remain non-tangible to the African countries. In 2003, four cotton-exporting countries (Benin, Burkina Faso, Chad and Mali) demanded that cotton subsidy removal be part of the WTO agriculture negotiations. The issue gained prominence at the Cancun Ministerial Conference in September 2003 with a number of NGOs conducting a high-profile campaign to bring attention to the difficulties faced by cotton producing developing countries.[27] Since then little progress has been made on removing subsidies on cotton. There is an urgent need to keep on fighting for the complete eradication of all forms of trade distorting subsidies on cotton and other commodities and to push on the debates towards the assumption of stricter commitments from the developed countries.

African proposal to level the playing field: Special and Differential Treatment
Consistent with Paragraph 44 of the Doha Declaration, African countries have tabled proposals in the current Doha negotiations relating to almost all the WTO Agreements under negotiations and review. In view of the fact that the special and differential treatment in the WTO Agreements is generally about best endeavours, expressed in imprecise and hortatory language and therefore, unenforceable before the WTO dispute settlement, African countries have called for members to make them legally binding. While there is an urgent need for making *special and differential treatments* (SDT) an integral part of the Agreements under negotiations, the need for the reduction of export subsidies and domestic support by the developed countries is even more serious.

African countries have also requested the unbundling of the four *Singapore issues* of competition policy, transparency in government procurement, trade facilitation and investment. On 27 and 28 of May 2004, African trade and finance ministers met in Kigali-Rwanda and took a common stand on the Doha negotiations, especially regarding the Singapore Issues. In the so-called 'Kigali Consensus' African countries requested members to drop all the Singapore Issues from the current Doha Development Round negotiations, with the exception of trade facilitation, which they regarded as critical for promoting intra-African trade and for harnessing the benefits of globalization.[28] They insisted that neither a multilateral agreement on trade facilitation and investment, competition nor transparency in government procurement would advance the development needs underlining the current Doha negotiations.

Life at the end of the road: Doha is dead!
It has been almost seven years since the 2001 Doha Conference of the WTO, which set out to "rebalance" the unbalanced Uruguay Round agreements. Due to unrelenting pressure by the developed countries, the Doha negotiations have veered from their proclaimed development orientation towards a 'market access' direction in which developing countries are pressurized to open up their agricultural, industrial and service sectors. In addition, the EU, Japan and the United Stated pledged to grant duty free ad quota free market access to 97 percent of the 50 least developed countries' products by 2008, with the exception of some 300 sensitive

26. See World Bank, 1999.
27. Baffes, 2005.
28. See TN/TF/W/33, available at http://docsonline.wto.org

products (such as sugar and rice) that are of interest to African countries.[29]

On the other hand, commitment was made by the US, EU and Japan at the Hong Kong ministerial trade talks in December 2005 to eliminate export subsidies on agricultural goods by the end of 2013. As of December 2006, no visible progress had been made on this front. Because these three giants wrote the WTO rules – creating loopholes that allows them to subsidize their farm economies – most subsidies have been 'repackaged' under any new WTO rules. The farm lobby and their congressional allies do not want to give up their existing subsidies, but they do want greater access to foreign markets, especially in developing countries. Considering that during the 2004 presidential election cycle, agribusiness industries contributed more than 53 million to political campaigns, it is not hard to see why.[30]

At the end of July 2006, the negotiations at the WTO on the Doha Work Programme were suspended across the board. Six WTO members (the US, the EU, India, Japan, Brazil and Australia) failed to bridge the gaps among themselves on the modalities of negotiations on two key areas: agriculture and non-agricultural market access (NAMA). The developed countries have succeeded in marginalizing the 'development issue', including the principles of special and differential treatment and less than full reciprocity in the agriculture and NAMA negotiations; not committing to reduce their total trade-distorting domestic subsidies beyond the actual levels; and by introducing new modalities in services which makes it potentially easier to pressure developing countries to liberalize while not making meaningful offers in areas that can practically benefit developing countries. In addition, they have succeeded in blocking progress in the TRIPS negotiations on disclosure of genetic resources and traditional knowledge. As one frustrated and courageous African president put it: "it is better to have no agreement than to walk away with a bad agreement".

Despite irreconcilable positions between developed and developing countries, the trade talks were restarted in mid-2008 in the hope of resolving the most contentious issues. This included basic issues of market assets, terms of trade distortions, commodity price volatility, fading out export subsidies in agricultural exports, and special and differential treatment for poor countries. Sadly after almost eight years of on and off negotiations, the Doha round of trade negotiations collapsed on the evening of 29 July 2008 when the developed countries refused to agree on a proposal to reduce their agricultural subsidies as well as to agree on a Special Safe-Guard Mechanism (SSM), that developing countries demanded in order to protect their farmers from sudden surge of agricultural imports.

It is important to note that trade, as an instrument for development and poverty eradication in Africa cannot be overemphasized. At the same time, it is to be acknowledged as well that while a favourable external environment is needed if African countries are to reap the benefits of their membership in the multilateral trading system, the supply-side constraints and the implementation of appropriate domestic measures by African governments in order to attract investment, must be addressed. As a consequence, if African countries are to compete effectively in the global market, they will need to implement the right policies and be supported to tackle their capacity constraints.

29. Das, Bhagirath Lal, 2006.
30. McNeely, 2006.

Africa and The European Union: From the Lome Convention to the Economic Partnership Agreements (EPAs)

In February 2000, the European Union and the African, Caribbean and Pacific countries concluded a new twenty-year partnership agreement that replaced the Lome Convention that used to be governed by a series of five-year 'Lome Conventions'. The Lome agreements provided trade preferences and aid to ACP countries, without requiring them to reciprocate. The ACP exporters were given substantial access to EU markets, while ACP countries retained the right to protect their producers from highly competitive (and often highly subsidized) EU exporters.

The last Lome Convention came to an end in 2000, and was replaced by the Cotonu Partnership Agreement, which had the principal objectives of reducing poverty and promoting the sustainable development of ACP countries and their gradual integration into the world economy.[31] Under the Cotonu Agreement, the EU and ACP agreed to maintain the Lome preferential system until the end of 2007, and then to replace it with a new Economic Partnership Agreement that would be WTO-compatible.

The EPA effectively scraps the Lome concessions in favour of liberal principles of open markets and global competitiveness. It further subordinates all African regional trade and integration arrangements to the WTO. The main elements of the agreement include:

- Rolling over non-reciprocal Lome trade preferences for eight years to 31 December 2007 under a waiver from the WTO
- No improvement in market access for the ACP into the EU market during the transitional period
- No firm commitment on maintenance during the transitional period of any protocol product, except sugar
- Introducing reciprocity from 2008 onwards in the form of free trade area between EU and ACP regions
- Produce trade agreements that are WTO-compatible.

With EPAs, the gains for the EU are clear; but it is hard to see where the gains will be for the ACP countries. Below we shall discuss three critical areas: market access gains; revenue gains; and regional integration.

Limited market access gains

Increased market access of ACP exports to the EU market is vaunted as one of the benefits of the EPAs. In reality however, the 39 least developed ACP countries will not gain appreciably from market access under an EPA since they have already been promised this access under the 'Everything but Arms' (EBA) programme for the least developed countries in 2001. Under the EBA, eligible countries have duty-free market access for the vast majority of their exports into the EU. For the remaining developing countries in ACP, it is unlikely that market access will be expanded beyond the preferences they already had under the Lome Conventions.

Market access is also undermined by other measures that amount to 'hidden forms of protectionism'. Even with an EPA, it is likely that ACP exports will continue to face stringent non-tariff barriers such as rules-of-origin, which limit the number of exports that can re-

---

31. Article 1 (2) of the Cotonou Agreement.

ceive preferential treatment;[32] the requirement of sanitary and phytosanitary (SPS) standards, which makes it very hard for their exporters to break into European markets; as well as other technical barriers attached to the trade preferences. Moreover, tariff escalation on key value chains, which levies higher taxes on processed goods (e.g. instant coffee) than on raw materials (such as coffee beans) deters ACP countries from processing their own products. In general, the protectionism facing African trade has been recently found to be "above the world average in spite of the trade preferences".[33]

Revenue loss

A substantial percentage of government revenue in many African countries is generated through tariffs levied on imports. The World Bank estimates that tariff revenues average between 7–10 percent of government revenues in sub-Saharan Africa.[34] The EU is the largest trading partner of many African countries. Consequently, the lion's share of this revenue comes from the duties imposed on imports from the EU. With the current EPA debates, wiping out tariffs on imports from the EU could have a damaging impact on government revenue in most of the sub-Saharan African countries. The United Nations Economic Commission (UNECA) for Africa in its 2005 report estimated the scale of revenue losses in sub-Saharan African countries with the full implementation of EPAs at US $ 1,951.3 million per annum.[35] This represents a level of income losses, which almost exceeds the total annual EU aid disbursement in Africa under the 9th European Development Fund (EDF). In the worst-case scenario, Gambia and Cape Verde stand to lose nearly 20 percent of their total government revenue, while Ghana and Senegal can be expected to face a decline in revenue of 10–15 percent.[36] Regrettably, the EU has not shown greater sensitivity to African concerns over the revenue and employment impacts of EPAs. These revenue losses will have a negative impact on the promised development dimension of EPAs – namely, poverty reduction.

Undermining of African regional integration

Regional integration is a central plank of the Cotonou Agreement and a key part of the development strategies of ACP countries.[37] However, if regional markets are opened to EU imports before they are consolidated, it will undermine rather than reinforce the regional efforts currently underway. In the case of SACU, SADC or CARIFORUM, for example, weaker and vulnerable economies are given differential treatment. The EPAs will effectively create a single regime with harmonized rules for all members so that EU exporters can enjoy a single point of entry. This is a direct challenge to regional governments' sovereignty in constructing their regional trade regime.

The Economic Partnership Agreement, as it is currently constituted, will not deliver their development promises. As shown above, the EPAs are not congruent with other key development commitments that the EU has made since 2000, including the EU-Africa strategy. The negotiations, both in process and content, were fraught with problems. Not only do

---

32. Rules of origin determine where a product 'comes from' for the sake of trade preferences, as only goods originating in certain countries qualify for duty-free access or lower tariffs. However, current rules are much stricter than necessary.
33. See Bigsten and Durevall, 2007.
34. Hinkle et al., 2005.
35. WITS/SMART Simulations cited in "The Economic and Welfare Impacts of the EU-Africa Economic Partnership Agreements", *ATPC briefing* No. 6, May 2005.
36. Busse et al., 2004.
37. Article 35 (2) emphasizes regional integration as a key instrument of ACP countries' integration into the world economy; while Article 37 (5) states that the negotiations will take into account the regional integration process within the ACP.

EPAs threaten existing productive sectors (both agriculture and manufacturing), they could severely undermine the ability of ACP governments to support future economic development. The removal of tariffs on EU imports will put products (often highly subsidized) from the EU in direct competition with products in some of the world's poorest countries. In 2005, for example the EU spent 1.43 billion Euro on export subsidies to dump surplus EU meat and dairy products on world markets, destroying livelihoods in some of the world's poorest countries.[38] The EU's own Sustainability Impact Assessment of EPAs argued that, 'While liberalization might encourage consumers to buy products at affordable prices, it might also accelerate the collapse of the modern West African manufacturing sector'.[39] The European Union has not lived up to its commitments and African rejection of the EPA in Lisbon in December 2007 is quite understandable.

Conclusion

In the final analysis, achieving the MDGs in Africa would require, at the very least, the introduction of mechanisms to achieve fair and stable prices for African commodities, improving market access for African exports, and removing western agricultural subsidies that put African producers at a disadvantage. Without action on agricultural subsidies by industrialized countries, Africa's development will always be held in check. In addition to rewriting the current global trade regime, new international measures are needed to strengthen the supply capacity of African countries in the commodity sector – especially in the area of production, marketing, and diversification to enhance value-added through processing and manufacturing based on commodities.[40] This must be complemented by domestic measures to overcome structural impediments in production. Thus, even if there is market access for these countries and developed countries' agricultural subsidies are removed, this 'supply constraint' will continue to prevent them from being able to take advantage of the access to western markets.

---

38. "Milking the CAP: How Europe's dairy regime is destroying livelihoods in the developing countries", *Oxfam International*, December 2002.
39. SIA of Trade Negotiations of the EU-ACP Economic Partnership Agreement, Mid-Term Report Working Draft, 1 October 2003. www.sia-gcc.org/acp/download/summarised_mid-term_report_final_doc_light.pdf
40. Khor, 2005.

5. Roadmaps to Africa's Renewal: Global and local dimensions

An ambitious and comprehensive approach is needed to tackle the interlocking problems impeding Africa's growth and development. This must involve diversification of products and markets, development of skills and human resources, modernization of technology and infrastructure, re-engineering of business processes, creation of incentives for small and medium enterprises to grow and export, improvement of country investment climate, and cultivation of foreign direct investment. Enhancing the investment climate entails government involvement within a wide area of governance – providing security, collecting taxes, ratifying sound economic policies into law, and delivering adequate public services. It also entails supporting the legal and financial institutional framework of the economy. The legal system must uphold order, act as a check on government and protect basic property rights, human rights, and contract rights. The financial system must promote household savings and channel them to productive enterprises.

This brings us back face to face with the issue of the role of the state in national development. Transformational change that moves African people to a higher standard of living requires the simultaneous, significant participation of the three major drivers of change: the state; the private sector and civil society. Without a healthy cohesion between these three actors, achieving the Millennium Development Goals and building peaceful and democratic societies will remain a dream. Experience shows that countries which have shaped a constructive, mutually supportive relationship between the public and private sectors have been more successful than those which have opted either for the primacy of the market or the predominance of the state.

An effective state maintains good policies and develops credible institutions that are supportive of growth. An effective state also strives for education and health systems which create a productive and skilled workforce, includes civil society in policy dialogue, and invests in the institutional and physical infrastructure to complement private dynamism. Therefore, strengthening state capacity becomes a sine qua non for Africa's economic and political renewal.

At the international level, the challenge of Africa's economic and political renewal will require a more auspicious international economic environment that would allow Africans to earn their way out of poverty. Key aspects in this regard should include: 'streamlining' conditionality, and bringing to a conclusion the Doha Development round of trade negotiations. With regard to the first, the common practice of lending with policy adjustment in the context of crisis management is not adequately governed by a set of policies and indicators that the countries themselves have specified to achieve development outcomes and monitor them accordingly. At the end of the day, for development in Africa to be sustainable, African governments must have the option to choose among appropriate fiscal, monetary, macroeconomic, trade and other economic and social policies without heavy-handed arm twisting by the development partners.

With regard to global trade rules, the big break for Africa has to come from progress in trade negotiations. One critical area is ending western agricultural subsidy and achieving fair and stable prices for commodities and improving access to African exports. This must be complemented by efforts to strengthen the supply capacity, especially in the area of production, marketing and diversification – to enhance the value-added of commodities through processing and manufacturing. This, of course, must be complemented by domestic measures to overcome constraints in production: access to credit, security of tenure, better transport and storage facilities.

A roadmap for Africa's development

The development challenge in Africa is multi-dimensional and conventional development orthodoxies are inadequate to address it. Central to Africa's renewal is the development of a strong, democratic and activist state that would assert its development role within the context of a common national vision. The lessons from China and East Asia in general demonstrate the importance of national policies, which support strategic industries, develop internal infrastructure, invest in human capital, and control financial markets. To carry this out, countries must have the ability, freedom and flexibility to make strategic choices unconstrained by the remote forces of globalization.

At the national level, there is an urgent need for African leaders to create an enabling policy environment to reverse the productivity failure in many sectors of the economy, and to build institutional capacity to respond appropriately to the demands of producers and consumers alike. Among the priorities are the following:

Reverse the productivity failure in agriculture

The disappointing economic performance of the continent over the past three decades has been caused, to a large extent, by the failure of African governments to create the proper conditions for an agricultural revolution to take place, which would in turn, propel the process of industrialization and social development. The priority task of an agricultural revolution that will remain for several decades to come, is obviously complex and multi-faceted. At the minimum, it requires the presence of a strong and effective 'enabling state', with the capacity to respond to the demand of rural producers. The state must play an active and supporting role by investing in agricultural research, extension, transport and communications and storage facilities which are essential factors for raising productivity and increasing the income of farmers. Government guaranteed prices and security of land tenure in particular are the most effective incentives that will shift peasant farmers from subsistence farming to production for the market.

Reverse the decline in higher education

Africa cannot flourish unless the intellectual capital of the continent is developed and maintained. Education is a cornerstone of human development in every society. Through education, people become aware of their environment and the social and economic options available to them. At the present moment, the state of education in Africa is pathetic. Despite tremendous gains made since the 1960s in increasing access to education, great challenges lie ahead. Spending on each child is half what it was 20 years ago. Perhaps the most daunting challenge is that of promoting female education. Fiscal crisis, poor student participation, high dropout and repetition levels, and low academic achievements are widespread destructive trends throughout the system.

An intellectual marginalization will occur unless Africa raises its educational levels and standards. The only way to narrow the knowledge gap is by investing in education, basic research and development. Strengthening African universities and preventing Africa's best and brightest from leaving the continent are important measures. Investment in education should emphasize the need to scale up the technological ladder and tap into the global system of information and knowledge. Transforming the African education system thus constitutes the second and most important pillar of the 'transformation' strategy.

Strengthening regional integration

Globalization, with its contradictory tendencies, poses a great challenge to African countries. Africa has been ill prepared to simultaneously adjust itself to complex global dynamics, exploit new opportunities or manage internal and external threats. Given the size of individual markets and the nature of their economies, a sub-regional problem-solving approach is an economic imperative – not just a political imperative. Selective strategic engagement with global forces (among which China is the latest force) from positions of greater collective economic and political strength within regional groupings is critical in order to improve gains from global engagement and minimize disadvantages. Such policies should support the goal of increased international competitiveness, for example, by promoting regional production chains and nurturing the development of regional markets in order to reduce demand-side constraints on growth.

Clearly, sub-Saharan African countries cannot easily jump into ambitious market integration schemes similar to the European Union, involving detailed blueprints, rigid time frames, and formal institutional structures, since the administration involved would require technical and managerial capacities that are not often found in sufficient quantity in Africa. One of the lessons from Africa's past experiment with regional integration is that less ambitious, more flexible institutional regional economic cooperation initiatives may have more potential because of their responsiveness to member states' priorities and interests. This implies less binding project-oriented and functional cooperation schemes involving action on certain themes or in certain sectors that offer some immediate benefits. These types of pragmatic institutional arrangements with realistic and well-defined objectives responding to specific short-term needs may offer better prospects than ambitious initiatives.

Expanding the governance reform agenda

One critical challenge in Africa today is how to make economic revitalization compatible with democracy. For democracy to succeed in the African context, however, it must go beyond instrumental aspects, such as the holding of multiparty elections. Democracy must translate into significant social reform and a reduction of inequalities as well as the decentralization of political power and decision-making. In the absence of real changes in people's lives, citizens can begin to regard democracy as an ideology of domination. Thus, by enlarging visions and raising consciousness, citizens can undermine the vicious circle of mass exclusion and marginalization.

Preventing deadly conflicts

If sustained peace is the goal, conflict resolution and post-conflict transformation must move beyond military response, and focus instead on addressing the root causes of conflict. At the most fundamental level, the absence of justice is frequently the principal reason for the absence of peace. Therefore, the principal objective of external and local efforts to prevent and resolve African conflicts should be the establishment of peace with justice.

Without this, efforts to resolve conflicts and rebuild societies are meaningless. Analysis and experience from other conflict-ridden parts of the world provide examples of a wide range of non-military means for resolving conflicts. These include: promoting confidence-building measures; establishing humanitarian norms and codes of conduct; establishing trust through cooperation on shared development problems and projects; and identifying specific mechanisms for sustaining peace initiatives. These options can only exist in a democratic environment. Thus the bond between peace and democracy must be strengthened.

Bibliography

Introduction

Adepoju, Aderanti, 2007, *Migration in Sub-Saharan Africa*, a contribution to the Swedish Government White Paper on Africa, The Nordic Africa Institute

Holmberg, Johan, 2007, *Natural Resources in sub-Saharan Africa: Assets and Vulnerabilities*, a contribution to the Swedish Government White Paper on Africa, the Nordic Africa Institute.

United Nations, 2006, 'African Migration: From tensions to solutions', *African Renewal*, 19(4):1.

1. Rural poverty, food insecurity and the struggle for resources

Bates, Robert, 1981, *Markets and States in Tropical Africa: The Political Bias of Agricultural Policies*. Berkley: University of California Press.

Bryceson, D.F., 2002, "The Scramble in Africa: Reorienting Rural Livelihoods", *World Development*, 30(5):725–39.

Butegwa, F., 1991, "Women's legal right of access to agricultural resources in Africa: A Preliminary Inquiry", *Third World Legal Studies,* pp. 45–47.

Chambers, Robert, 1991, The State and Rural Development: *Ideologies and an Agenda for the 1990s.* IDS Discussion Paper 269, University of Sussex.

Cousins, Ben, 2007, "Land and Agrarian Reform in the 21st Century: Changing Realities, Changing Arguments?" Keynote address, Global Assembly of Members, International Land Coalition, Entebbe, Uganda, 24–27 April 2007.

Havnevik, Kjell, Lars Erik Birgegård, Deborah Bryceson, Prosper Matondi and Atakilte Beyene (eds), 2007, *Agriculture toward Poverty Alleviation or Impoverishment?* Policy Dialogue No.1. Uppsala: The Nordic Africa Institute.

Lentz, Carola, 2006, "Land Rights and the Politics of Belonging in Africa: An Introduction", in Kuba, Richard and Carola Lentz (eds), *Land and the Politics of Belonging in West Africa*. London and Boston: Brill, pp. 1–34.

Rigg, Jonathon, 2006, "Land, farming, livelihoods and poverty: Rethinking the links in the rural South", *World Development,* Vol. 34, No. 12, pp. 180–202.

Rutherford, Blair, 2007, Commentary on Henry Bernstein's paper at Research Forum on "New Agrarian Questions in Africa", Nordic Africa Institute, Uppsala, 4 May 2007.

World Bank, 1981, *Accelerated Development for Sub-Saharan Africa: An Agenda for Action*. Washington DC: World Bank.

World Bank, 2008, *World Development Report – Agriculture for Development*. Washington DC: World Bank.

2. The urban challenge in Africa

Amis, Philip, 1995, "Making Sense of Urban Poverty", *Environment and Urbanization*, Vol. 7, No.1, pp. 145–157.

Amis, P., 2004, "Regulating the informal sector: Voice and bad governance", in Devas, N. (ed.), *Urban Governance, Voice and Poverty in the Developing World*. London: Earthscan.

Attahi, Kofi, 1989, "Côte d'Ivoire: An evaluation of urban management reforms", in Stren, R. and R. White (eds), *African Cities in Crisis*. Boulder: Westview Press, pp. 112–146.

Baker, Jonathan, 1992, *Small Towns in Africa*. Uppsala: The Scandinavian Institute of African Studies.

Beall, Jo, 2002, "Globalization and Social Exclusion in Cities: Framing the debate with lessons from Africa and Asia", *Environment and Urbanization,* Vol. 14, No.1, pp. 41–51

Becker, C.A. Hamer, and A. Morrison, 1994, *Beyond Urban Bias in Africa.* Portsmouth, NH: Heinemann.

Bromley, Ray, 1978, "Introduction: The Urban Informal Sector: Why it is worth discussing?" *World Development,* Vol. 6, Nos. 9/10, pp. 1033–9.

Brown, A. (ed.), 2006, *Contested Space: Street Trading, Public Space, and Livelihoods in Developing Cities.* Warwickshire: ITDG Publishing.

Bubba, Ndina and Lamba, Davinder, 1991, "Local government in Kenya", *Environment and Urbanization,* Vol. 3, No. 1, pp. 37–59.

Cairnacross, Sandy et al. (1990), *The Poor Die Young: Housing and Health in the Third World,* London: Earthscan.

Cheru, Fantu, 1989, *The Silent Revolution in Africa: Debt, Development and Democracy.* London and Harare: Zed Books.

Cheru, Fantu, 1992, "Social Dimensions of Economic Reform: Proposals to Initiate Urban Community-Based Rehabilitation in the Major Towns of Ethiopia", Addis Ababa, mimeo.

Davis, J. et al., 2003, "Corruption in public service delivery: Experience from South Asia's water and sanitation sector", *World Development,* 32(1).

De Soto, Hernando, 1989, *The Other Path: The Invisible Revolution in the Third World.* New York: Harper & Row.

Devas, N. (ed.), 2004, *Urban Governance, Voice and Poverty in the Developing World.* London: Earthscan.

Gilbert, Alan and Gugler, Josef, 1992, *Cities, Poverty and Development.* Oxford: Oxford University Press.

Global Water Partnerships, 2003, *Financing Water for All.* Report of the World Panel on Financing Water Infrastructure, chaired by Michel Camdessus (March 2003).

Gugler, J., 2002, "The son of the hawk does not remain abroad: The urban-rural connection in Africa", *African Studies Review* 45, pp. 21–41.

Halfani, M., 1989, "Empowering people and building communities" in Stren, R. and R. White (eds), *African Cities in Crisis: Managing Rapid Urban Growth.* Boulder: Westview Press.

Hansen, K. and M. Vaa (eds), 2004, Reconsidering Informality: *Perspectives from Urban Africa.* Uppsala: The Nordic Africa Institute, pp. 62–80.

Hoogevelt, A., 1997, *Globalization and the Postcolonial World: The New Political Economy of Development.* London: Macmillan.

ILO (1973), *Employment, Incomes and Equality: A Strategy for Increasing Productive Employment in Kenya.* Geneva: ILO.

IMF/Paris21, 2000, *A Better World for Us All – Progress towards the International Development Targets.* A joint publication of IMF, UN, OECD and the World Bank Group

Jaglin, Sylvy, 2002, "The right to water versus cost recovery: Participation, urban water supply and the poor in sub-Saharan Africa", *Environment and Urbanization,* Vol. 14, No. 1, pp. 231–245.

Jamal, Vali and John Weeks, 1988, "The Vanishing Rural-Urban Gap in Sub-Saharan Africa", *International Labor Review,* Vol. 127, No. 3, pp. 271–292.

Kuluba, Saitiel,1989, "Local Government and Management of Urban Services in Tanzania", in Stren, R. and R. White (eds), *African Cities in Crisis: Managing Rapid Urban Growth.* Boulder: Westview Press, pp. 203–245.

Lee-Smith, D. and R. Stren, 1991, "New Perspectives on African Urban Management", *Environment and Urbanization,* Vol. 3, No. 1, pp. 23–36.

Le Pere, Garth, Kato Lambrechts and Anthoni van Nieuwkerk, 1999, "The Burden of the Future: South Africa's Foreign Policy Challenges in the New Millennium", *Global Dialogue,* Vol. 4, No. 3, pp. 3–8.

Levey, Caren, 1992, "Gender and the environment: The challenge of crosscutting issues in Development Policy Planning", *Environment and Urbanization*, Vol. 4, No. 1, pp. 134–149.

Lipton, Michael, 1997, *Why Poor People Stay Poor: The Urban Bias in Public Policy*, Cambridge MA: Harvard University Press.

Lugalla, J., 1997, "Development, change and poverty in the informal sector during the era of structural adjustment in Tanzania", *Canadian Journal of African Studies*, 31:3.

Mitlin, D., 2004, "Civil society organisations: Do they make a difference to urban poverty?" in Devas, N. (ed.), *Urban Governance, Voice and Poverty in the Developing World*. London: Earthscan.

Moser, Caroline, 1995, "Urban Social Policy and Poverty Reduction", *Environment and Development*, Vol. 7, No. 1, pp. 159–171.

Obudho, Robert A. and Sala El-Shaks (eds), 1975, *Urbanization, National Development, and Regional Planning in Africa*. New York: Praeger.

Onibokun, Adepoju, 1989, "Urban Growth and Urban Management in Nigeria", in Stren, R. and R. White (eds), *African Cities in Crisis: Managing Rapid Urban Growth*, Boulder: Westview Press, pp. 68–111.

Pruss, Annette, David Kay, L. Fewtrell, Jamie Bartram, 2002, "Estimating the burden of disease from water, sanitation and hygiene at a global level", *Environment and Health Perspectives*, Vol. 110, No. 5, pp. 537–542.

Rakodi, C. and T. Lloyd-Jones (eds), 2002, *Urban livelihoods: A people-centred approach to reducing poverty*. London: Earthscan

Ray, Kalyan, 2000, "Water for Thirsty Cities", *Habitat Debate*, Vol. 6, No. 3.

Rees, William E., 1999, "Achieving Sustainability: Reform or Transformation?" in Satterthwaite, David (ed.), *The Earthscan Reader in Sustainable Cities*. London: Earthscan, pp.22–52

Satterthwaite, David, 1995, "The underestimation and misinterpretation of urban poverty", *Environment and Urbanization,* Vol. 7, No. 1, pp. 3–10

Shi, A., 2000, "How Access to Urban Potable Water and Sewerage Connections Affects Child Mortality", Development Research Group. Washington DC: World Bank.

Silva, G., N. Tynan and Y. Yilmaz, 1998, "Private participation in the water and sewerage sector: Recent Trends", *Public Policy for the Private Sector*, Note No. 147, August.

Simone, A. and A. Abouhani (eds), 2005, *Urban Africa: Changing Contours of Survival in the City*. Dakar: CODESRIA Books.

Sparr, Pamela (ed.), 1994, *Mortgaging Women's Lives: Feminist Critique of Structural Adjustment*. London: Zed Books.

Strange, Susan, 1996, *The Retreat of the State: The Diffusion of Power in the World Economy*. Cambridge University Press.

Stren, Richard, 1989, "The administration of urban services", in Stren, R. and R. White (eds), *African Cities in Crisis*. Boulder: Westview Press, pp. 36–37

UNDP, 1991, *Cities, People and Poverty: A UNDP Strategy Paper*. New York: UNDP.

UN-Habitat, 2003, *Water and Sanitation for the World's Cities*. London: Earthscan.

UN-Habitat, 2003, *The Challenge of Slums*. London: Earthscan, p. 216.

UN-Habitat, 2006, *The State of the World's Cities Report 2006–7*. London: Earthscan

UNICEF/WHO, 2000, *Global Water Supply and Sanitation Assessment 2000 Report*. Joint Monitoring Program. New York: United Nations.

UNICEF/WHO, 2004, *Meeting the MDG Drinking Water and Sanitation Target: A Mid-Term Assessment of Progress,* (August 2004). New York: United Nations.

Warah, Rasna, 2000, "Nairobi Descends into Darkness and Despair", *Habitat Debate*, Vol. 6, No. 3, pp. 8–9.

Wratten, Ellen, 1995, "Conceptualizing Urban Poverty", *Environment and Urbanization*, Vol. 7, No. 1, pp. 11–36.

Woldemicael, G.K., 2000, "The Effects of water supply and sanitation on childhood mortality in urban Eritrea", *Journal of Biosocial Science*, Vol. 32, No. 2, pp. 207–227.

World Bank, 1991, *Urban Policy and Economic Development: An Agenda for the 1990s.* Washington DC: World Bank.

World Bank, 1993, *Water Resources Management Policy Paper.* Washington DC: World Bank.

World Commission on Environment and Development, 1987, "The Urban Challenge", in *Our Common Future.* New York: Oxford University Press.

Yared, Tadesse, 1996, "Solid waste management in peri-urban areas of Ethiopia", *Water and Sanitation News,* Vol. 3 (September–December).

3. Conflict prevention and post-conflict transformation

Adelman, Howard and Astri Suhrke (eds), 1999, *Path of Genocide: The Rwandan Crisis from Uganda to Zaire.* Piscataway, NJ: Transactions Publishers.

Annan, Kofi, 1989, *The Causes of Conflict and the Promotion of Durable Peace and Sustainable Development in Africa.* Report of the Secretary-General to the Security Council, S/1998/318, April 13.

Aronoff, Yael S., 1998, "An Apology Is Not Enough", *Washington Post,* 9 April, P. A25.

Baker, Jonathan, and Tade Akin Aina (eds), 1995, *The Migration Experience in Africa*, Uppsala: Nordiska Afrikainstitutet.

Boutros-Ghali, Boutros, 1992, *An Agenda for Peace.* Report of the Secretary-General to the Security Council, S/24111, June 17.

Bush, Kenneth, 1996, "Beyond Bungee Cord Humanitarianism: Towards a Democratic Agenda for Peace Building", *Canadian Journal of Development Studies,* 17, pp. 75–92

Buur, Lars, Steffen Jensen and Finn Steppurat (eds), 2006, *The Security-Development Nexus. Expressions of Sovereignty and Security in Southern Africa*, Uppsala: Nordiska Afrikainstitutet.

Bøås, Morten, and Kevin C. Dunn, 2007, *African guerrillas: Raging against the machine.* Boulder CO: Lynne Rienner.

Cheru, Fantu, 2001, 'Building War Torn Societies', in Cheru, F., *African Renaissance: Roadmaps to the Challenge of Globalization.* London: Zed Press, pp. 210–218.

Duffield, Mark, 2002, "War as a Network Enterprise: The New Security Terrain and Its Implications", *Cultural Values*, Vol. 6, No. 1&2, pp. 153–165.

Human Rights Watch/Africa Watch, 1997, *Liberia: Emerging from the Destruction.* New York: Human Rights Watch.

Kaldor, Mary, 1999, *New and Old Wars: Organised Violence in a Global Era.* Cambridge: Polity Press.

Kaplan, Robert, 1994, "The Coming Anarchy", *Atlantic Monthly,* February, p. 34.

Kwesi Aning, 2007, "Africa Confronting Complex Threats: Coping with Crisis", International Peace Academy, Working Paper Series (February).

Lederach, John, 1995, *Preparing for Peace: Conflict Transformation across Cultures.* Syracuse NY: Syracuse University Press.

MacGaffey, Janet, et al., 1991, *The Real Economy of Zaire. The Contribution of Smuggling and Other Unofficial Activities to National Wealth.* London: James Currey and Philadelphia: University of Pennsylvania Press.

Nabudere, D., 2004, "Africa's First World War: Mineral Wealth, Conflicts and War in the Great Lakes Region", Pretoria: *AAPS Occasional Paper Series,* Vol. 8, No. 1.

Obi, Cyril, 2006a, "Terrorism in West Africa: Real, emerging and imagined threats?", *African Security Review,* Vol. 15, No. 3, pp. 87–101.

Obi, Cyril, 2006b, "Foreign Interests and Environmental Degradation", in Rothchild, D. and E. Keller (eds), *Africa-US Relations: Strategic Encounters.* Boulder CO: Lynne Rienner.

Paris, Roland, 2002, "International peace building and the 'mission civilisatrice'", *Review of International Studies,* 28, pp. 637–656.

Richards, Paul (ed.), 2005, *No peace – no war: Anthropology of contemporary armed conflicts.* Oxford: James Currey.

Turton, David, 2003, "Conceptualising Forced Migration", *Refugee Studies Centre Working Paper,* No. 12. University of Oxford: Queen Elizabeth House, International Development Centre.

Utas, Mats, 2003, *Sweet Battlefields: Youth and the Liberian Civil War* (PhD thesis). Uppsala: Dissertations in Cultural Anthropology (DiCA), Department of Cultural Anthropology and Ethnology, Uppsala University.

World Bank, 2000, *Can Africa Claim the 21st Century?* Washington DC: World Bank, p. 30.

4. Africa and the World Trading System: The challenge of 'rebalancing' the 'unbalanced rules'

Baffes, J., 2005, "The Cotton Problem", *World Bank Research Observer,* 20(1):109–144.

Bigsten, Arne and Dick Durevall, 2007, *The African economy and its role in the world economy,* a contribution to the Swedish Government White Paper on Africa, the Nordic Africa Institute.

Bilal, S. and F. Rampa, 2006, "Alternative (to) EPAs: Possible scenarios for the future ACP trade relations with the EU", ECDPM, *Policy Management Report 11,* February.

Busse, M. et al., 2004, "The Impact of ACP/EU Economic Partnership Agreements on ECOWAS Countries: An Empirical Analysis of the Trade and Budget Effects", Institut für Wirtschaftsforschung, Hamburg.

Das, Bhagirath Lal, 2006, "Why the EU and the US offers on farm trade are not good enough", TWN Briefing Paper 33.

Dollard, D. and A. Kraay, 2002, "Spreading the Wealth", *Foreign Affairs,* January/February.

Fortucci, Paola, 2003, "The Contributions of Cotton to Economy and Food Security in Developing Countries", United Nations Food and Agriculture Organization (FAO), June 2003.

Gomory, Ralph E. and William J. Baumol, 2000, *Global Trade and Conflicting National Interests.* Cambridge, MA: The MIT Press.

Hinkle, L. et al., 2005, "Beyond Cotonou: Economic Partnership Agreements in Africa", in Newfarmer, R., *Trade, Doha, and Development: A window into the issues.* Washington DC: The World Bank, pp. 267–80.

Kessie, Edwina, 2000, "Enforceability of the Legal Provisions Relating to Special and Differential Treatment under the WTO Agreements", *The Journal of World Intellectual Property,* Volume 3, Issue 6:955–975.

Kessie, Edwini, and Yvonne Apea, 2004, "The Participation of African Countries in the Multilateral Trading System", *African Yearbook of International Law,* Vol. 12, pp. 9–66.

Khor, Martin, 2001, *Rethinking Globalization: Critical Issues and Policy Choices.* London: Zed Press.

Khor, Martin, 2004, "Comments on the WTO's Geneva 'July 2004 Package'", *Third World Network Briefing Paper 22.* Penang, Malaysia: TWN, August.

Khor, Martin, 2005, "The commodities crisis and the global trade in agriculture: Present problems and some proposals", in Cheru, F. and C. Bradford (eds), *Millennium Development Goals: Raising the Resources to Tackle World Poverty*. London: Zed Press and Helsinki Process, pp. 97–117.

McNeely, Kathy, 2006, "Food Security and Trade in Agriculture: Africa keeps a watchful eye on US policy", *Washington Notes on Africa*, Vol. 31, No. 1, p. 7.

Ngangjoh, Yenkong H., 2005, "Disputing Trade Preferences at the WTO Dispute Settlement Body: Revisiting the EC/ACP Sugar Preferences", *Estey Centre Journal of International Law and Trade Policy,* Vol. 6, No. 2, pp. 148–180.

Perkins, Francis, 2003, "Africa's Agricultural Trade Reform and Development Options", *Trade Policy Briefing*, No. 1, South African Institute of International Affairs.

World Bank, 1999, *Cotton Policy Brief,* June 1999. Washington DC: World Bank.

World Bank, 2000, *Can Africa Claim the 21st Century?* Washington DC: World Bank.

World Trade Organization, 2002, *The Legal Texts, The Results of the Uruguay Round of Multilateral Trade Negotiations*. Cambridge: Cambridge University Press.

World Trade Organization, 2004, *World Trade Report 2004*, Prospects for 2005. Press/401; 14 April 2005.

World Trade Organization, 2005, *World Trade Report 2004*, Prospects for 2005. Press/401; 14 April 2005.

CURRENT AFRICAN ISSUES PUBLISHED BY THE INSTITUTE
Recent issues in the series are available electronically
for download free of charge www.nai.uu.se

1. *South Africa, the West and the Frontline States. Report from a Seminar.* 1981, 34 pp, (out-of print)

2. Maja Naur, *Social and Organisational Change in Libya.* 1982, 33 pp, (out-of print)

3. *Peasants and Agricultural Production in Africa. A Nordic Research Seminar. Follow-up Reports and Discussions.* 1981, 34 pp, (out-of print)

4. Ray Bush & S. Kibble, *Destabilisation in Southern Africa, an Overview.* 1985, 48 pp, (out-of print)

5. Bertil Egerö, *Mozambique and the Southern African Struggle for Liberation.* 1985, 29 pp, (out-of print)

6. Carol B.Thompson, *Regional Economic Polic under Crisis Condition. Southern African Development.* 1986, 34 pp, (out-of print)

7. Inge Tvedten, *The War in Angola, Internal Conditions for Peace and Recovery.* 1989, 14 pp, (out-of print)

8. Patrick Wilmot, *Nigeria's Southern Africa Policy 1960–1988.* 1989, 15 pp, (out-of print)

9. Jonathan Baker, *Perestroika for Ethiopia: In Search of the End of the Rainbow?* 1990, 21 pp, (out-of print)

10. Horace Campbell, *The Siege of Cuito Cuanavale.* 1990, 35 pp, (out-of print)

11. Maria Bongartz, *The Civil War in Somalia. Its genesis and dynamics.* 1991, 26 pp, (out-of print)

12. Shadrack B.O. Gutto, *Human and People's Rights in Africa. Myths, Realities and Prospects.* 1991, 26 pp, (out-of print)

13. Said Chikhi, Algeria. *From Mass Rebellion to Workers' Protest.* 1991, 23 pp, (out-of print)

14. Bertil Odén, *Namibia's Economic Links to South Africa.* 1991, 43 pp, (out-of print)

15. Cervenka Zdenek, *African National Congress Meets Eastern Europe. A Dialogue on Common Experiences.* 1992, 49 pp, ISBN 91-7106-337-4, (out-of print)

16. Diallo Garba, *Mauritania–The Other Apartheid?* 1993, 75 pp, ISBN 91-7106-339-0, (out-of print)

17. Zdenek Cervenka and Colin Legum, *Can National Dialogue Break the Power of Terror in Burundi?* 1994, 30 pp, ISBN 91-7106-353-6, (out-of print)

18. Erik Nordberg and Uno Winblad, *Urban Environmental Health and Hygiene in Sub-Saharan Africa.* 1994, 26 pp, ISBN 91-7106-364-1, (out-of print)

19. Chris Dunton and Mai Palmberg, *Human Rights and Homosexuality in Southern Africa.* 1996, 48 pp, ISBN 91-7106-402-8, (out-of print)

20. Georges Nzongola-Ntalaja *From Zaire to the Democratic Republic of the Congo.* 1998, 18 pp, ISBN 91-7106-424-9, (out-of print)

21. Filip Reyntjens, *Talking or Fighting? Political Evolution in Rwanda and Burundi, 1998–1999.* 1999, 27 pp, ISBN 91-7106-454-0, SEK 80.-

22. Herbert Weiss, *War and Peace in the Democratic Republic of the Congo.* 1999, 28 pp, ISBN 91-7106-458-3, SEK 80,-

23. Filip Reyntjens, *Small States in an Unstable Region – Rwanda and Burundi, 1999–2000,* 2000, 24 pp, ISBN 91-7106-463-X, (out-of print)

24. Filip Reyntjens, *Again at the Crossroads: Rwanda and Burundi, 2000–2001.* 2001, 25 pp, ISBN 91-7106-483-4, (out-of print)

25. Henning Melber, *The New African Initiative and the African Union. A Preliminary Assessment and Documentation.* 2001, 36 pp, ISBN 91-7106-486-9, (out-of print)

26. Dahilon Yassin Mohamoda, *Nile Basin Cooperation. A Review of the Literature.* 2003, 39 pp, ISBN 91-7106-512-1, SEK 90,-

27. Henning Melber (ed.), *Media, Public Discourse and Political Contestation in Zimbabwe.* 2004, 39 pp, ISBN 91-7106-534-2, SEK 90,-

28. Georges Nzongola-Ntalaja, *From Zaire to the Democratic Republic of the Congo.* Second and Revised Edition. 2004, 23 pp, ISBN-91-7106-538-5, (out-of print)

29. Henning Melber (ed.), *Trade, Development, Cooperation – What Future for Africa?* 2005, 44 pp, ISBN 91-7106-544-X, SEK 90,-

30. Kaniye S.A. Ebeku, *The Succession of Faure Gnassingbe to the Togolese Presidency – An International Law Perspective.* 2005, 32 pp, ISBN 91-7106-554-7, SEK 90,-

31. Jeffrey V. Lazarus, Catrine Christiansen, Lise Rosendal Østergaard, Lisa Ann Richey, *Models for Life – Advancing antiretroviral therapy in sub-Saharan Africa.* 2005, 33 pp, ISBN 91-7106-556-3, SEK 90,-

32. Charles Manga Fombad and Zein Kebonang, *AU, NEPAD and the APRM – Democratisation Efforts Explored.* Edited by Henning Melber. 2006, 56 pp, ISBN 91-7106-569-5, SEK 90,-

33. Pedro Pinto Leite, Claes Olsson, Magnus Schöldtz, Toby Shelley, Pål Wrange, Hans Corell and Karin Scheele, *The Western Sahara Conflict – The Role of Natural Resources in Decolonization.* Edited by Claes Olsson. 2006, 32 pp, ISBN 91-7106-571-7, SEK 90,-

34. Jassey, Katja and Stella Nyanzi, *How to Be a "Proper" Woman in the Times of HIV and AIDS.* 2007, 35 pp, ISBN 91-7106-574-1, SEK 90,-

35. Lee, Margaret, Henning Melber, Sanusha Naidu and Ian Taylor, *China in Africa.* Compiled by Henning Melber. 2007, 47 pp, ISBN 978-91-7106-589-6, SEK 90,-

36. Nathaniel King, *Conflict as Integration. Youth Aspiration to Personhood in the Teleology of Sierra Leone's 'Senseless War'.* 2007, 32 pp, ISBN 978-91-7106-604-6, SEK 90,-

37. Aderanti Adepoju, *Migration in sub-Saharan Africa.* 2008. 70 pp, ISBN 978-91-7106-620-6 SEK 90,-

38. Bo Malmberg, *Demography and the development potential of sub-Saharan Africa.* 2008, 39 pp, 978-91-7106-621-3, SEK 90,-

39. Johan Holmberg, *Natural resources in sub-Saharan Africa: Assets and vulnerabilities.* 2008, 52 pp, 978-91-7106-624-4, SEK 90,-

40. Arne Bigsten and Dick Durevall, *The African economy and its role in the world economy.* 2008, 66 pp, 978-91-7106-625-1, SEK 90,-

41. Fantu Cheru, *Africa's development in the 21st century: Reshaping the research agenda.* 2008, 47 pp, 978-91-7106-628-2, SEK 90,-

www.ingramcontent.com/pod-product-compliance
Lightning Source LLC
Chambersburg PA
CBHW080057280326
41934CB00014B/3349